TABLE OF CONTENTS

A Study Guide

Explorations in Microeconomics

First Canadian Edition

Rocky M. Mirza
James F. Willis
Martin L. Primack

CAT Publishing Company

ISBN 1-56226-058-8

PREFACE

The function of any study guide is to help you review the subjects covered in the basic textbook in a variety of ways. When you approach the materials again and again, from several different angles, the ideas begin to rub off on you. You get the repetition that helps to fix in your mind the knowledge that the authors consider important. That is why we prepared this study guide, as a supplement to the Mirza/Willis/Primack text, *Explorations in Microeconomics.*

We assume, to begin with, that you're going to read over a given chapter in the text from start to finish, marking those portions you think you may want to come back to later. Mark liberally, and jot in the margin any notes you think may help you. In this way you will make the text act as a notebook for the course. Then turn to the study guide.

Each unit of the study guide presents exercises for a chapter and its accompanying application(s), and is divided into four parts. Part 1 first asks that you *reread* the summaries given at the end of the chapter and application. Then Part 1 briefly outlines the chapter and application in a general way, pointing out the core ideas. It lists those concepts you must grasp if you are to have an adequate understanding of the principles of economics. Terms defined in the text's Glossary are in boldface for your reference.

Part 2 lists new terms and concepts, and asks you to define them. You need not write out these definitions; just mentally phrase them. If you feel unable to define a term accurately, look back at the section in the text in which the term is introduced or check the text's Glossary. Reread the definition until you think you've got a handle on the concept. Then go back over the list later, when the material has had time to get cold. In economics, definitions are very important.

Part 3 leads you through the material once again, by asking you to answer essay questions. Sometimes you are also asked to do a short series of problems or arithmetic exercises. (The level of math required is no higher than simple algebra.) Often, answers are provided in the Answers section at the end of the unit.

Part 4 is a self-test, with all the answers provided at the end of the unit. The self-test takes three forms: (1) true/false questions, which you should answer with the proviso that you have a clear idea of *why* you picked the answer you did; (2) multiple-choice questions; and (3) matching questions. This self-test section will give you a pretty clear idea of how well you understand the subject matter. Answer the questions first; *then* check your answers against the key. You should get at least 80 percent right.

Your instructor may use this study guide as a part of the instructional program, and may make assignments in it. You may, however, simply use this guide in a program of self-study.

Rocky M. Mirza
James F. Willis
Martin L. Primack

CHAPTER 1 *Breaking the Ice*

Application 1 *Self-interest: Endangered Motivation or the Key to the Future?*

PART 1

Reread the sections entitled "Summing Up" at the end of Chapter 1 and Application 1. These summaries offer an excellent review of both chapter and application.

Things to Watch For

Chapter 1

Economics—originally called "political economy"—has existed as a separate area of study for about two centuries. Early economists (called classical economists), beginning with Adam Smith, were generally pessimistic about the future of people's material well-being. Twentieth-century economists are much more optimistic about the ability of society to manage or even, in the long run, to solve economic problems. By economic problems, they mean the ability of a society to provide for the material well-being of its people.

Chapter 1 defines economics, describes the methods used by economists, and discusses why a knowledge of those methods is important. The definition of economics emphasizes these basic facts: (1) Economics is a social (rather than a physical) science. (2) It is analytical rather than simply descriptive. (3) It is concerned with the material well-being of people.

Chapter 1 explains that economists seek to analyze world problems by a method that ordinarily encompasses three stages: (1) A *descriptive* stage, in which economists gather the facts that bear on the causes of the problem. (2) A *theorizing* stage, in which economists formulate a **model**, or a simplified set of relationships that form an analogy to reality. In this stage they may also formulate a hypothesis—that is, assume a certain relationship between variables contained in the model—and then test the model to see to what extent a change in the "problem" variable can be explained by changes in the other variables stated in the hypothesis. (3) A *policy-making* stage, when economists know the results of the testing and are prepared to make recommendations on an *economic policy*. Bear in mind that economic policies are a part of overall social policies; economists themselves rarely make those policies.

As you study economics, always be aware that the principles you learn won't lead you to *unique* conclusions about solutions to economic problems. Not even experienced professional economists have *unique* solutions to the world's problems.

Throughout the text you will find sections called applications. These applications are short articles about economic problems. Each is designed to illuminate the economic theory you have learned in the preceding chapter. You will find that you are already familiar with most of these problems; the only new thing will be the approach, or the *way* the problem is treated, using economic principles. Each time you finish an application, consider how those principles may be applied to other problems you are aware of. You will be surprised at how universally applicable the tools of the economist are.

When you get to the end of a chapter or application, carefully read the summary of it, entitled "Summing Up," which gives a point-by-point list of the main things to remember.

As you work your way through the book, don't be anxious about how much mathematics you are expected to know. A major feature of this book is its mathematical simplicity. We believe that a student can learn basic principles of economics and how to apply them, without having calculus or any of the other mathematical tools that are useful in advanced economics courses. We do, however, make extensive use of graphs as visual illustrations of economic relationships. The combination of verbal explanations and graphical illustrations will reinforce your understanding of both principles and problems.

Application 1

Application 1 deals with the question: What motivations underlie people's economic behavior? It traces the efforts of economists, ever since the eighteenth century's Adam Smith, to answer this question. Smith said that self-interest is the dominant motivation of people. He maintained that the role of government should be to make sure that the self-interested efforts of private citizens contribute as much as possible to the public interest. Benthamites (nineteenth-century followers of Jeremy Bentham) believed that humans are walking calculators of pain and pleasure, and that all they want is to maximize pleasure (a view known as hedonism).

Later economists, such as Alfred Marshall, rejected the notion of precise maximization of pleasure, but continued to believe that the pursuit of monetary gain, as well as the satisfaction to be derived from consuming the goods bought with money, is people's most powerful economic motivation. John Maynard Keynes, writing in the 1930s, observed that the economic problem—scarcity and the limits it imposes on satisfying human wants—might be solved. However, he felt that until scarcity could be eliminated, nations would have to continue to rely on human self interest to create savings, investment, and growth. Most modern economists agree that self-interest, although not the *only* economic motivation, is the most powerful one. They feel that business firms *almost* maximize profits and consumers *almost* maximize satisfaction.

Radical economists maintain that **Homo communista** (communist man) will replace the old idea of the self-interested **Homo economicus** (economic man). The communist citizen, they say, will be concerned with the interests of the group and the community as a whole, not with the interests of self.

PART 2

Define the following terms and concepts.

1. Hedonism
2. Model
3. Hypothesis
4. Economic problem
5. Positive economics
6. Normative economics

PART 3

Answer the following questions and problems.

1. How has the view of people's economic motivation changed over the last hundred years?

2. Why did nineteenth-century philosophers call economics "the dismal science"? What has happened to make it less dismal in the twentieth century?

3. What are the three basic stages in economic analysis? What is the role of the economist in the third stage?

4. Using Figure 1-1, do the following things:
   a. Label the axes on which one measures changes in the dependent variable and the independent variable.
   b. Draw "curves," showing (1) an inverse relationship between the two variables; (2) a direct relationship between them; (3) a curve that is positively sloped; (4) a curve that is negatively sloped; (5) a curve in which all change is in the dependent variable; and (6) a curve in which all change is in the independent variable. Label the curves 1, 2, 3, and so on.

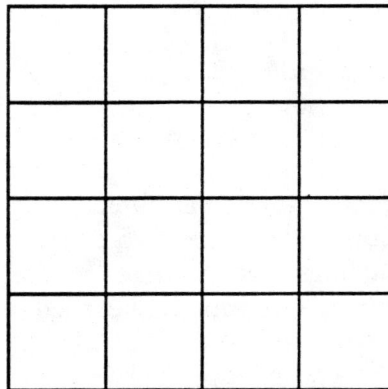

Figure 1-1 Graph for Problem 4

PART 4 Self-test

SECTION A True/false questions

T   F   1. Unless businesses exactly maximize profits and consumers exactly maximize satisfaction, self-interest is ruled out as an economic motivation.

T   F   2. If a curve is positively sloped, there is a *direct* relationship between the dependent and independent variables.

T   F   3. A model exactly describes reality.

T   F   4. A hypothesis is a statement of relationships that are known to be true.

T   F   5. Economists can generally create controlled laboratory conditions that permit them to repeat laboratory experiments dealing with economic behavior.

T   F   6. Economists assume that material problems are the only important problems.

T   F   7. In order to make economic policy, a person must be an economist.

T   F   8. Economists are generally more optimistic today about the *ability* of people to solve problems of material well-being than they were 150 years ago.

T   F   9. All economists assume that business firms maximize profits to the greatest degree possible.

T   F   10. Most economists accept the old assumption of *Homo economicus* as an appropriate way to explain the behavior of consumers and producers.

SECTION B Multiple-choice questions

1. Which one of the following do most economists *not* assume to be true of economic behavior?
   a. Consumers and producers have clear objectives.
   b. Consumers seek to obtain as much satisfaction as possible.
   c. Producers seek to obtain as much profit as possible.
   d. Consumers and producers are more concerned with the interests of others than with their own interests.

2. Which of the following statements is *positive*?
   a. We should break up all large corporations.
   b. Consumers ought to be represented in the Cabinet.
   c. Unions are bad.
   d. The deficit in the federal budget last year was about $200 billion.

3. Which of the following statements is *normative*?
   a. American Telephone and Telegraph (AT&T) earned 9.6 percent on its investment last year.
   b. There are more telephones in the United States than in any other nation.
   c. New telephones put into service last year numbered 200,000.
   d. The breakup of AT&T into several companies was a good decision.

4. Adam Smith believed that the public interest is best served by
   a. government planning.
   b. monopolistic firms.
   c. wage-price controls.
   d. self-interest harnessed to the public good.

5. Alfred Marshall argued that the economic motive of people is to achieve
   a. a contemplative life.
   b. power over others.
   c. monetary gain.
   d. subjective social welfare.

6. John Kenneth Galbraith believes that most economic decisions are made by
   a. profit-maximizing, independent business people.
   b. corporate technocrats.
   c. satisfaction-maximizing consumers.
   d. government wage-price planners.

7. Marxists seek to discredit *Homo economicus* because they believe that, in a capitalist society,
   a. concentration of power in the hands of business firms leads to alienation of workers and consumers.
   b. business people are concerned with social welfare.
   c. government prevents maximization of profit and satisfaction.
   d. people don't have enough information to act rationally.

8. A positively sloped curve is one that
   a. slopes up to the right.
   b. slopes down to the left.
   c. involves an inverse relationship between two variables.
   d. expresses no clear relationship between variables.

9. Which of the following is *not* a characteristic of economics?
   a. It is analytical.
   b. It is a social science.
   c. It deals with material relationships.
   d. It deals mostly with things that cannot be quantified.

10. The economist's method is based on all but which one of the following?
    a. Gathering of facts
    b. Model building
    c. Transcendental meditation
    d. Hypothesizing

SECTION C Matching questions

Match the phrases in column B to the terms in column A.

Column A	Column B
1. Model	(a) Assumed relationship(s)
2. Positive statement	(b) Analogy to reality
3. Inverse relation	(c) Self-satisfaction
4. Hypothesis	(d) What *should* be
5. *Homo communista*	(e) What *is*
6. Direct relationship	(f) Mankind interested in self
7. Hedonism	(g) Mankind interested in the community
8. Economic problem	(h) Limits imposed by scarcity
9. Normative statement	(i) Independent and dependent variables move in opposite directions
10. *Homo economicus*	(j) Independent and dependent variables move in the same direction.

ANSWERS

Part 4

Section A 1, F; 2, T; 3, F; 4, F; 5, F; 6, F; 7, F; 8, T; 9, F; 10,T
Section B 1, *d*; 2, *d*; 3, *d*; 4, *d*; 5, *c*; 6, *b*; 7, *a*; 8, *a*; 9, *d*; 10, *c*
Section C 1, b; 2, e; 3, i; 4, a; 5, g; 6, j; 7, c; 8, h; 9, d; 10, f

CHAPTER 2   *Scarcity and the Production Possibilities Curve*

PART 1

Reread the section entitled "Summing Up" at the end of Chapter 2. This summary offers an excellent review of the chapter.

Things to Watch For

Chapter 2

Chapter 2 starts off with a discussion of markets. A market system is a set of means by which buyer-seller exchanges are made. The invisible hand argument proposed by Adam Smith indicates that the self-interest decisions of buyers-sellers can make everyone better off through the actions of markets (the invisible hand).

The rest of the chapter deals with scarcity and its relationship to economic development and to the making of economic decisions. Scarcity is the relationship between limited resources and unlimited human wants. Because of scarcity, societies cannot satisfy all wants for goods and services. They must devise means by which to choose which goods to produce and who is to get them.

In a capitalist society, which allows private ownership of the means of production, economic questions relating to scarcity are answered through a system of *markets*, the medium through which buyer-seller exchanges are made. These questions, then, are common to all societies: (1) *What* goods shall be produced? (2) *How* shall they be produced? (3) *For whom* shall they be produced? If it were not for scarcity, all goods and services would be available to everyone. Furthermore, they would be free; that is, they would have no price. Scarcity, though, exists in all societies at all times. Thus people must find solutions to these three interdependent questions.

Answering questions involves making choices. One way for a society to view its economic choices is through the device of the **production-possibilities** function, a relationship showing the combinations of goods and services that a society, at full employment and using all its resources according to the best available technology, can produce during a given period of time. When one graphs these choices, the resulting curve is called a **production-possibilities curve** (PP curve). The PP curve represents a frontier or outer limit to a society's productive capacity.

However, neither the production-possibilities function nor the PP curve can tell us what combinations of goods and services a society will actually choose to produce. Each nation must establish its own means for making these choices. The means a society uses may range from letting markets alone dictate the choices to turning the responsibility over to a group of government bureaucrats. Most societies use some combination of these two means.

A production-possibilities curve is a useful device for understanding various aspects of employment. **Employment** is the condition in which a unit of resource (land, labor, capital, or entrepreneurship) is used in an economic activity. **Full employment**, exists when all units find uses. **Unemployment** exists when there are units of resources that cannot find uses within an economic system. Underemployment exists when resources find some employment, but in activities that are less than their most productive uses.

Full employment, in terms of the production-possibilities curve, means that a nation is on that curve, its production frontier. Underemployment or unemployment means being below the curve. (In Canada, it is conventional to define full employment as no more than seven percent unemployment; this allows for people who are between jobs.)

In a developing society, the production-possibilities curve naturally shifts from time to time. The choices a society makes now will influence its PP curve in the future. If it chooses to produce more capital (heavy machinery, factories, and so on) now, it will experience more growth or shift in productivity in the future than if it chooses more consumer goods now and gives up a certain amount of growth in productivity in the future.

Production-possibilities curves are usually drawn as bowed or concave to the origin of a graph. This reflects an assumption of *increasing opportunity cost*. **Opportunity cost** means the alternative goods you give up when you choose to produce a certain thing. (For example, a society may forgo the opportunity to produce a certain number of tractors in order to put up some needed low-cost housing.) Economists usually assume that opportunity cost ultimately increases in any society. In other words, a society will gradually give up more and more of one thing in order to produce more and more of another. Gradually, it will opt for specialization of its resources. Now land, labor, and capital are more productive when used to produce some things than when used to produce others. This means that a society that expands its output of one good will finally begin to use, in a specialized way, resources that would have been more productive if used in some other way. So the society ultimately experiences a **diminishing rate of transformation**, or rate at which one good may be substituted for another.

Economic institutions—the social arrangements through which economic decisions are made—have a lot to do with which choices a society makes about using its resources, and also with how well the decisions are carried out.

PART 2

Define the following terms and concepts.

1. Market system
2. Resources
3. Scarcity
4. Free goods
5. Production-possibilities function
6. Employment-unemployment-underemployment
7. Opportunity cost
8. Rate of transformation
9. Diminishing rate of transformation
10. Economic institutions
11. Property rights
12. Entrepreneurship

PART 3

Answer the following questions and problems.

1. What is meant by the "Invisible Hand?" How can it make people better off?

2. What kind of economy would exist for you and for other people in a world without scarcity? Would you want or have a job in such a world?

3. Can scarcity and affluence exist at the same time for the same people?

4. Why must all economies devise a means for answering the basic economic questions of what to produce, how to produce, and who is to get the output?

5. Consider the hypothetical production-possibilities schedule in Table 2-1.
   a. Use Figure 2-1 to plot the production-possibilities curve of India from the data in Table 2-1.
   b. What is the rate of transformation from points B to C?
   c. What happens to the rate of transformation? Why?
   d. What would the rate of transformation look like if all resources used in producing wheat and trucks were equally productive in either use?

Table 2-1 Production Possibilities for Wheat and Trucks, India

Product	Production Rates				
	A	B	C	D	E
Wheat (thousands of tons)	0	20	40	60	80
Trucks (thousands)	60	53	38	20	0

6. What factors could shift the production-possibilities curve in Figure 2-1?

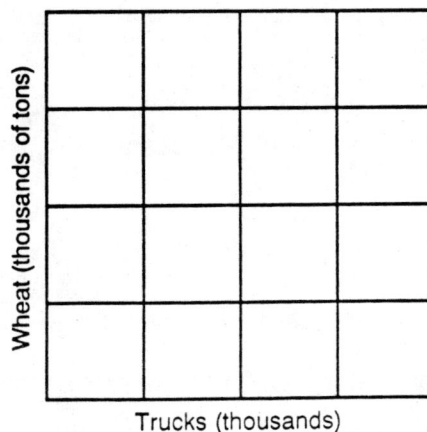

Figure 2-1 Production Possibilities

7. Draw points in Figure 2-1 that correspond to positions of
   a. full employment.
   b. underemployment.

PART 4 Self-test

SECTION A True/false questions

T   F   1. The "Invisible Hand" is the watchful eye of a benevolent government.

T   F   2. If jobs can be found for everybody in the labor force, underemployment will be eliminated.

T   F   3. A nation is usually on its production-possibilities curve.

T   F   4. If resources are not specialized at all, a production-possibilities "curve" will be a straight line.

T   F   5. Opportunity cost is likely ultimately to increase for any nation.

T   F   6. The reason why nations experience a diminishing rate of transformation is that societies don't make wise choices about how to use resources.

T   F   7. Labor productivity tends to increase with increased specialization.

T   F   8. The production-possibilities curve of Canada has shifted greatly in the twentieth century.

SECTION B Multiple-choice questions

1. Which one of the following best fits the idea of Adam Smith's "Invisible Hand"?
   a. Actions of God-favoring market economies
   b. Actions of a benevolent government making the right choices for the people
   c. Actions of buyers and sellers in a market environment that maximizes the benefit from markets
   d. Central planning in the Soviet Union

2. Which one of the following is *not* a reason why we need a means of allocating resources?
   a. Scarcity
   b. Limited resources
   c. Unlimited wants
   d. Low incomes

3. Which one of the following is *not* a basic question confronting all economic societies?
   a. What shall be produced?
   b. How should markets be made competitive?
   c. For whom shall goods be produced?
   d. How is output to be produced?

4. Which of the following is *not* necessarily one of the benefits of economic development?
   a. Higher per capita incomes
   b. More happiness
   c. More freedom of choice
   d. More leisure

5. Which one of the following is *not* one of the fundamental factors necessary for shifting a nation's production-possibilities curve?
   a. Economic integration
   b. Technological change
   c. Decreasing opportunity cost
   d. Basic structural or institutional change

SECTION C Matching questions

Match the phrases in Column B to the terms in column A.

Column A	Column B
1. Economic integration	(a) Resource paid same price in all uses
2. Basic economic questions	(b) Buyer-seller exchanges
3. Economic development	(c) Limited resources, unlimited wants
4. Entrepreneurship	(d) Zero price
5. Market system	(e) Growing real per capita income
6. Production-possibilities curve	(f) What we give up to produce something
7. Opportunity cost	(g) Organization of diverse resources
8. Scarcity	(h) Land, labor, capital, and entrepreneurship
9. Resources	(i) What, how, for whom
10. Free goods	(j) Output frontier or limit

ANSWERS

Part 4

Section A 1, F; 2, F; 3, F; 4, T; 5, T; 6, F; 7, T; 8, T
Section B 1, c; 2, d; 3, b; 4, b; 5, c
Section C 1, a; 2, i; 3, e; 4, g; 5, b; 6, j; 7, f; 8, c; 9, h; 10, d

CHAPTER 3   *Supply and Demand: Price Determination in Competitive Markets*

Application 3   *When Should We Let Supply and Demand Work? Rent Controls and the Price of Housing*

PART 1

Reread the sections entitled "Summing Up" at the end of Chapter 3 and Application 3. They constitute an excellent review of both the chapter and the application.

Things to Watch For

Chapter 3

This chapter deals with how prices are set in a competitive (that is, a free, private-enterprise) capitalist economy. **Competition** is the market form in which individual buyers and sellers have no influence over the price at which they buy and sell. Price in such a market is determined by the independent influences of supply and demand.

    Demand is a set of relationships showing the quantities of a good that consumers will buy over a range of prices within a specific period of time. The factors that determine the demand for a good are (1) the price of that good (the main factor), (2) incomes of buyers, (3) tastes and preferences of buyers, (4) prices of other products (both *complements*, which are goods used in conjunction with another product, and *substitutes*, which are used in place of another product), and (5) consumers' expectations about future prices and market conditions. These five factors determine an individual's demand. Total demand for a good (or for all goods) is influenced by a sixth factor as well: the number of consumers, or the population.

    One may establish a hypothetical **demand curve** for a good by holding constant all variables influencing the demand for that good except its price. (This is the *ceteris paribus*, or other-things-being-equal, assumption.) The resulting demand schedule or curve (when plotted) reflects the facts that (1) people buy more of a good at low prices than at high prices (the **law of demand**), (2) there is a price above which consumers drop out of the market, and (3) the strength of a person's taste for a good probably declines as the person gets more of it.

    A demand curve ordinarily slopes down to the right. This happens for two reasons. (1) As the price of a good falls, consumers buy more of it and substitute the good for other, relatively more expensive ones (**substitution effect**). (2) As the price of a good falls, consumers' purchasing power increases, so they buy more of that good (**income effect**).

Exceptions to the downward-sloping demand curve are rare. They include (1) goods that are so very **income-inferior** that people buy less of them as their price falls and use their increased purchasing power to buy other, more desired goods (for example, beans in a poor country), and (2) **Veblen goods**, goods that have greater appeal to consumers at higher prices than at lower prices (perhaps super yachts).

Learn the difference between a **change in demand** and a **change in quantity demanded**. A change in demand involves a shift of the demand curve. It arises from a change in income, tastes, prices of other goods, people's expectations, or number of consumers. A change in the quantity demanded involves a movement along a demand curve. It may be caused only by a change in the price of the good itself. (A change in the quantity of eggs demanded can be caused only by a change in the price of eggs.)

To arrive at a schedule for market demand, one sums up the demand curves of individuals. Generally, economists assume that there are no interdependencies between the demand curves of individuals. Thus the adding up is simple. (Occasionally, though, people jump on a bandwagon. They rush out to buy a Frisbee, or some such thing, because someone else has one. In such a case, the process of adding up can become complicated.) At any rate, the curves depicting market demand, like the curves depicting individual demand, usually slope downward to the right.

The other side of the market is **supply**. Supply is a set of relationships showing the quantities of output that a firm will offer for sale at each possible price within a specific period of time. Supply is determined by (1) the price of the good, (2) the technology used to produce it, (3) prices of inputs or resources, (4) prices of other goods, and (5) the firm's expectations about future prices.

Learn the difference between a **change in supply** and a **change in quantity supplied**. A change in supply involves a shift of the supply curve. It may be caused by (1) a change in technology, (2) a change in prices of inputs, (3) a change in the price of other goods, or (4) a change in the firm's expectations about future prices. A change in the quantity supplied involves a movement along the supply curve and may be caused only by a change in the price of the good itself. (When the price of cars goes up, the quantity of cars supplied goes up as a result.)

A supply schedule, when plotted, is called a **supply curve**. According to the **law of supply**, supply curves slope up to the right. When prices are high, firms offer to sell larger quantities than they do when prices are low.

To arrive at a schedule for market supply, one sums up the supply curves of individual firms. As in the case of demand, the adding up assumes that there are no interdependencies (that is, no collusion) between firms. For competitive suppliers this assumption works well, since no single firm has any influence over price or any reason to observe what another firm is doing.

Prices are established by the forces of supply and demand, which operate jointly but —under competition—independently of each other. An **equilibrium price** is a price at which quantity supplied equals quantity demanded.

A *dis*equilibrium price may be either higher or lower than the equilibrium price. If a price is higher, there is **excess supply**. Firms offer to sell more than consumers want to buy, or more than they can buy. If a price is lower than equilibrium, there is **excess demand**. Consumers want to buy more than firms have available to sell. Therefore, an equilibrium price is a market-clearing price. It is a price that eliminates excess supply or demand.

The final point in Chapter 3 concerns the conditions necessary for competitive pricing: (1) flexible prices, with no floors or ceilings, (2) full information on the part of buyers and sellers, (3) expectations that prices will hold constant in the future, (4) free entry into and exit from the industry (mobility of resources), (5) maximizing of profit by firms and maximizing of satisfaction by consumers, and (6) absence of conspiracies or collusion.

Application 3

This application discusses effects of government established prices in general and, more specifically, government imposed rent controls. Rent controls create a disequilibrium and, in this case, an excess demand. With a price fixed below the equilibrium, quantity demanded increases and quantity supplied may decrease. The quality of housing will also probably decline.

The application discusses who gains and who loses and why.

The best case with rent control exists where supply is perfectly inelastic (a vertical line). Excess demand occurs because of the increase in quantity demanded under the lower controlled rent. The worse case exists where supply slopes up and excess demand occurs because of both increases in quantity demanded and decrease in quantity supplied with a lower than equilibrium (controlled) rent. If rent control also reduces supply or shifts the supply curve to the left, excess demand is even greater.

PART 2

Define the following terms and concepts.

1. Competition
2. Demand
3. Change in demand
4. Change in quantity demanded
5. *Ceteris paribus* assumption
6. Income-inferior goods
7. Veblen goods
8. Income effect
9. Substitution effect
10. Supply
11. Change in supply
12. Change in quantity supplied
13. Law of demand
14. Law of supply
15. Aggregation
16. Equilibrium price
17. Excess demand
18. Excess supply

PART 3

Answer the following questions and problems.

1. What conditions must exist in order for a market to function competitively? Is it easy to create these conditions? Why?

2. In an economy that grows rapidly for a long period of time, what is the most important factor affecting demand? Why is this so?

3. In an economy that grows rapidly, what factor has the strongest influence on supply? Why?

4. Evaluate the following statement: The only thing that *can't* cause a change in the demand for gasoline is a change in the price of gasoline.

5. Explain fully the difference between demand and quantity demanded and between supply and quantity supplied. Give examples of these differences and illustrate with appropriate graphs.

6. Consider Figure 3-1 and do the following things:
   a. Label both axes properly.
   b. Label the demand curve and the supply curve.
   c. Label the equilibrium price.
   d. What does one call the distance CD? Label it.
   e. What does one call the distance AB? Label it.
   f. Why is the equilibrium price the price that tends to be created?

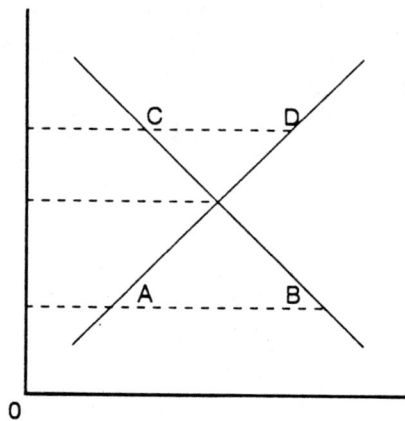

Figure 3-1 Equilibrium Pricing

7. In November 1975, the Associated Press reported the following: The owners of the New Orleans Sandwich Shop in Seattle, Washington, found that when they priced their hot dogs (reportedly the Rolls-Royce of the tube steaks) at $1.00 each, "sales were awful." When they raised the price to $1.45, sales doubled. When they raised the price to $1.75, sales doubled again!
   a. Draw a diagram to show what the demand curve for these hot dogs apparently looked like.
   b. Can you think of a reason why sales rose as price increased?
   c. What term do economists use for a good such as this one?
   d. The New Orleans Sandwich Shop slipped into oblivion when the Frankfurter opened down the street and sold hot dogs for 70 cents. Why?

8. For most goods, would the income effect or the substitution effect of a price change have a greater influence on the change in quantity demanded? Why?

9. Draw the diagram of a housing market that has a perfectly inelastic supply with a downward sloping demand curve. Indicate excess demand under rent control. Do the same for a case in which the supply of housing is upward sloping and the demand downward sloping; indicate the increase in excess demand. What happens to excess demand when the supply of housing decreases?

10. use supply/demand analysis to illustrate the effect of the GST on the price of restaurant meals.

PART 4 Self-test

SECTION A True/false questions

T   F   1. In the case of most goods, rising incomes cause the quantity demanded to increase.

T   F   2. Veblen goods probably appeal to the snobbishness of people.

T   F   3. If the price of a good goes up, the demand for it decreases.

T   F   4. If the price of butter goes up, the demand for margarine is likely to increase, since margarine is a *substitute* for butter.

T   F   5. If the price of automobiles rises, the demand for tires is likely to fall, since the two are *complementary* products.

T   F   6. It probably won't take much of an increase in the price of gasoline to decrease the demand for gasoline.

T   F   7. One person's demand curve is likely to be very much like another person's.

T   F   8. If the price of video tapes goes up, the quantity of them that is supplied will increase.

T   F   9. The law of supply tells us that price of a good and quantity supplied are inversely related.

T   F   10. Market solutions to economic problems involve using price to ration output.

T   F   11. When supply is perfectly inelastic, rent controls lead to excess demand *solely* because of the increase in quantity demanded.

SECTION B Multiple-choice questions

1. In a competitive market, all but which one of the following conditions exist?
   a. Full knowledge on the part of buyers and sellers
   b. Price flexibility
   c. Absence of collusion
   d. Barriers to free entry and exit

2. Demand depends on all but which one of the following?
   a. Tastes and preferences of buyers
   b. Prices of complements and substitutes
   c. Incomes of buyers
   d. The existence of competitive market conditions

3. Supply depends on all but which one of the following?
   a. Income
   b. Prices of other goods
   c. Technology of production
   d. Prices of inputs

4. *Complementarity* is illustrated by which one of the following?
   a. Demand for bread increases as price of margarine falls.
   b. Demand for pizzas rises as price of hamburgers increases.
   c. Demand for used cars decreases as price of new cars falls.
   d. Demand for mass transit increases as price of gasoline rises.

5. *Substitutability* is illustrated by which one of the following?
   a. Demand for recreational facilities rises as income increases.
   b. Quantity of housing demanded falls as price of housing rises.
   c. Demand for beer increases as the price of whiskey increases.
   d. Demand for paint increases as the price of housing decreases.

6. Which one of the following is *not* a characteristic of equilibrium price?
   a. Quantity supplied equals quantity demanded.
   b. Excess supply equals zero.
   c. Price never changes.
   d. Excess demand equals zero.

7. Demand curves normally slope down to the right because of all but one of the following factors. Which?
   a. Law of demand
   b. Veblen-goods effect
   c. Substitution effect
   d. Income effect

8. Which one of the following is least likely to be an income-inferior good?
   a. Beans
   b. Rice
   c. Education
   d. Corn

9. Which of the following is *not* true about rent controls?
   a. Quantity demanded increases
   b. Quantity supplied may increase
   c. Quality may decrease
   d. Excess supply appears

10. Which of the following is true about rent controls?
    a. Most economists favor rent controls
    b. Governments use it because it subsidizes landlords
    c. Those who live in rent controlled housing are strong political supporters of such legislation
    d. All those who wish to rent are benefitted by rent control

11. Which of the following will generate the most excess demand in rent controlled situations?
    a. Perfectly inelastic supply
    b. Upward sloping supply
    c. Uncharged demand
    d. Reduced supply and downward sloping demand

SECTION C Matching questions

Match the phrases in column B to the terms in column A.

Column A	Column B
1. Equilibrium price	(a) No influence over price
2. Inferior good	(b) Quantity demanded falls as price falls
3. Change in demand	(c) Other things being equal
4. Monopolistic pricing	(d) People buy more of one good as price of other goods fall
5. Expectations	(e) People buy more as price increases
6. Competition	(f) Market clearing
7. Veblen good	(g) Shift of demand curve
8. *Ceteris paribus*	(h) Cartel
9. Upward-sloping curve	(i) Future prices
10. Complementarity	(j) Price and quantity directly related

ANSWERS

PART 4

Section A   1, F; 2, T; 3, F; 4, T; 5, T; 6, F; 7, F; 8, T; 9, F; 10, T; 11, F
Section B   1, *d*; 2, *d*; 3, *a*; 4, *a*; 5, *c*; 6, *c*; 7, *b*; 8, *c*; 9, *d*; 10, *c*; 11, *d*
Section C   1, f; 2, b; 3, g; 4, h; 5, i; 6, a; 7, e; 8, c; 9, j; 10, d

CHAPTER 4   *The Demand Side of the Market*

Application 4   *Will Redistributing Income Make People Happier?*

PART 1

Reread the section entitled "Summing Up" at the end of Chapter 4 and Application 4. It provides an excellent review of both the chapter and the application.

Things to Watch For

Chapter 4

Chapter 4 deals with **demand,** the set of relationships that reveals how much of a good consumers will buy over a range of prices within a given period of time. Economists' models of demand usually depend on the following assumptions: (1) Consumers know about and can choose among alternatives. (2) Consumers seek maximum satisfaction from the goods they buy with their limited incomes. (3) Factors other than the price of a good that might influence demand (income, tastes, prices of other goods, expectations of future prices, number of consumers) do not vary in the time period for which demand is established.

A hypothetical demand schedule for a good reflects the **law of demand,** which says that price and quantity demanded are inversely related (an increase in price results in a decrease in quantity demanded; a decrease in price results in an increase in quantity demanded).

There are various ways to explain demand. Chapter 4 offers two theories as bases for explaining consumer behavior: (1) utility theory, which is based on the degree of satisfaction consumers get from various combinations of goods; and (2) the income and substitution effects of a change in prices on consumers, that is, indifference curves analysis.

When we draw a graph of a demand schedule that obeys the law of demand, we obtain a downward-sloping curve. A decrease in the price of a good causes an increase in the quantity demanded for two reasons. First is the **income effect,** or the change in quantity demanded caused by the increase in purchasing power due to a fall in price. Second is the **substitution effect,** the change in quantity demanded resulting from the substitution of the now relatively cheaper good for other, relatively more expensive goods. The substitution effect *generally causes* a downward-sloping demand curve. Since consumers can almost always find substitutes, quantity demanded tends to change in a direction opposite to that of a price change. The income effect, on the other hand, usually *reinforces* a downward-sloping curve. As the price of a good falls and people have more purchasing power, they buy more of that good if it is considered desirable. The two effects, then, validate the law of demand.

However, this law may not hold for a class of goods called *income-inferior goods;* which are goods for which the income effect of a price change may work just opposite from the way it's described above: as the price of a strongly income-inferior good, called a **Giffen good**, falls, people buy *less* of that good and more of some other, more desirable good. Ordinarily, the substitution effect is more important than the income effect. (A change in the price of *one* good doesn't change consumers' purchasing power very much.) But if the income effect is stronger than the substitution effect, the net effect of a price decrease may be to cause consumers to buy less of a good.

Another exception to the law of demand is the **Veblen good**. This is a good that consumers buy more of at high prices than at low prices. Such goods (perhaps caviar, furs, and so on) have snob appeal.

Utility theory is another means of explaining consumer behavior. Utility, or satisfaction, is measured in *utils*. Economists assume that consumers (1) buy competitively, (2) have limited incomes but full information, (3) are rational and seek to accomplish their objectives, and (4) seek to maximize total utility within the limits of their money incomes.

The **law of diminishing marginal utility** holds that beyond some point, the additions to utility (**marginal utility**, or MU) that arise from consuming a particular good decrease (in a given period of time). Building on this principle, and on the assumption that consumers try to get the maximum utility permitted by their incomes, economists set forth the following as being the set of conditions necessary to achieve maximum utility:

1. $$\frac{MU_a}{P_a} = \frac{MU_b}{P_b}$$

2. $P_aA + P_bB$ = income

where A = the amount of good A, B = the amount of good B, P_a = price of A, and P_b = price of B.

Condition 1 says that the marginal utility per dollar spent on good A should equal the marginal utility per dollar spent on good B. If this were not so, you would get more satisfaction by spending less on one good and more on the other. You could gain more utils than you would lose. Your best position is the one in which you can't change from one good to the other and get any net addition to your utils or satisfaction. Condition 2 simply says that what you spend on good A (P_a times the amount of A bought, or P_aA) plus the amount you spend on good B (P_aB) must equal your income. In other words condition 2 says that you live within (or on) your income, or that you have a **budget restraint**.

Each point on the individual's demand curve must fulfill the above two conditions. Suppose that a consumer is in equilibrium. The consumer equates the marginal utility of a dollar spent on one good with the MU of a dollar spent on the other good (condition 1) and spends all his or her income on good A plus good B (condition 2). Now suppose that the price of good A falls (the price of good B does not change). The consumer will substitute the relatively cheaper good (A) for the relatively more expensive one (B). Thus the consumer gains the MU of a dollar more spent on A. But in spending less on the other good (B), the consumer loses the MU per dollar that would have been spent on it. In this way (assuming that good A is a desirable good), the consumer will increase the quantity of good A demanded until MU_a/P_a is again equal to MU_b/P_b. Using these two equilibrium conditions, we can establish as many points as needed on the demand curve.

One thing the preceding argument suggests is that prices of goods and quantities of them demanded are established in terms of their marginal rather than their total utility. This leads to the **paradox of value,** which is that consumers pay higher prices for goods whose total utility is small but whose marginal utility is great (diamonds) than for goods whose total utility is great but whose marginal utility is small (water).

Once we establish demand curves for individuals, we can establish demand curves for markets. To find market demand, we add the demand curves of individuals (assuming that there are no interdependencies, such as "keeping up with the Joneses").

It is often important to know how responsive the quantity demanded is to changes in price. The measure of the rate at which quantity demanded changes as price changes is called the **price elasticity of demand.** Demand may be (1) **price elastic,** in which case quantity demanded changes at a faster rate than price; (2) **price inelastic,** in which case quantity demanded changes at a slower rate than price; or (3) **unit elastic,** in which case quantity demanded changes at the same rate as price.

The usual formula for measuring price elasticity of demand (E_d) is:

$$E_d = \frac{\text{percentage change in quantity demanded}}{\text{percentage change in price}}$$

$$= \frac{\Delta Q/Q}{\Delta P/P} = \frac{[Q_2 - Q_1]/[(Q_1 + Q_2)/2]}{[P_2 - P_1]/[(P_1 + P_2)/2]}$$

(This **midpoint formula** gives us the average rate of change in quantity and price between two prices and quantities.) In figuring elasticity we ignore the minus sign, because is has no economic significance.

The three broad degrees of elasticity can also be determined by changes in total revenue. If, as price falls, demand is elastic, quantity demanded increases by a greater percent than price and total revenue increases. If, as price falls, demand is inelastic, quantity demanded increases by a smaller percent than price and total revenue decreases. If, as price falls, demand is unit elastic, quantity demanded increases at the same rate as price and total revenue is unchanged. For price increases, thus, total revenue declines if demand is elastic, total revenue increases if demand is inelastic and total revenue is unchanged if demand in unit elastic.

Demand not only may be price elastic, price inelastic, or unit elastic; it also may be characterized by two extremes. (1) in the case of **perfect inelasticity,** $E_d = 0$, and when price changes, the quantity demanded does not change at all. (2) In the case of **perfect elasticity,** $E_d \rightarrow \infty$, when quantity demanded changes, the price does not change at all.

Note: Any straight-line demand curves other than those reflecting the two above extremes have varying elasticities throughout their length.

Four things determine the price elasticity of demand for a good: (1) *Substitutability.* If there are good substitutes for a commodity, the demand for it tends to be elastic. (2) *Proportion of income spent on the good.* If consumers spend a significant part of their incomes on the good, demand for it tends to be elastic. (3) *Postponability.* If one can easily postpone the consumption of a good, demand for it tends to be elastic. (4) *Time.* The longer the period of time the more one can adjust to price changes and the more elastic demand tends to be.

There are many concepts of elasticity other than the price elasticity of demand. One is the income elasticity of demand, the rate at which the demand for a good varies as consumers' incomes vary. This is helpful in identifying normal goods, inferior goods, or superior goods. Another is cross price elasticity of demand, the rate of change in the demand for one good divided by the rate of change in the price of another good. This measures the degree of complementarity and substitutability between goods.

Application 4

Application 4 deals with the relationships between changes in income and changes in total utility or satisfaction. It does not deal with happiness, since economists don't know any more than anyone else what makes people happy. They can, however, hypothesize various relationships between income changes and utility changes.

The most common hypothesis is that of **diminishing marginal utility of income**. This hypothesis states that beyond some income level, further additions to income yield smaller and smaller increments of utility. There are two alternative hypotheses: (1) *Constant marginal utility of income.* Each addition to income adds the same amount of utility. (2) **Increasing marginal utility of income.** Each addition to income adds increasing amounts of utility.

In the absence of machines to record changes in people's utility or satisfaction, most economists accept the diminishing-marginal-utility-of-income hypothesis. Whichever hypothesis they accept, they usually assume that people's assessments of the utility they derive from added income are the same. Then they set forth the following arguments about redistributing income to increase total utility. (1) *Diminishing MU of income.* If income is redistributed from upper-income groups to lower-income groups, total utility will grow, since the utility lost by the rich is smaller than the utility gained by the poor. (2) *Constant MU of income.* No gain in total utility is possible from a redistribution of income, since one group's gain of utility will exactly offset the other's loss of utility. (3) *Increasing MU of income.* Total utility could be increased by redistributing income in favor of upper-income groups, since the utility gained by the rich would more than offset the utility lost by the poor.

Data show that between 1935 and 1970, income distribution in the United States became more nearly equal. From 1970 through 1985, the distribution of income trends have been reversed. The upper income groups, especially the highest five percent, has increased its share while the lowest 60 percent has significantly declined in its share of total income.

Application 4 makes two warnings: (1) Government can play a big role in redistributing income. In the United States, government has done this through transfer payments, food stamps, job training, and many other programs. (2) Redistributing income does not affect only the utility of the nation's consumers. It may have effects on morals, on aggregate demand, on incentives (to save, to invest, to make efforts in certain directions, and so forth).

As you might have suspected, the application suggests that economic theory points to no single "best" distribution of income.

PART 2

Define the following terms and concepts.

1. Demand
2. Law of demand
3. Income effect
4. Substitution effect
5. Veblen good
6. Giffen good
7. Utility theory
8. Law of diminishing marginal utility
9. Normal goods, superior goods, inferior goods
10. Budget restraint
11. Market demand
12. Price elasticity of demand
13. Price elastic, price inelastic, unit elastic
14. Independent utilities
15. Midpoint formula
16. Income elasticity of demand
17. Cross price elasticity of demand

PART 3

Answer the following questions and problems.

1. What do economists assume when they are constructing a model of demand? Why are these assumptions necessary?

2. Which would you expect to be more important usually: the income effect, or the substitution effect? Why?

3. Are there any goods that are income inferior to you? If so, what makes them income inferior?

4. Are any goods Veblen goods to you? If so, why are they so?

5. What conditions of utility theory are fulfilled at all points on an individual's demand curve?

6. Consider Tables 4-1 (a) and (b) which detail the utility situations of a consumer whose total income is $10.50 and who must choose between buying stereo cassettes and magazines. (A = number of cassettes or magazines bought; B = dollars spent on cassettes or magazines; C = marginal utility of cassettes or magazines; D = marginal utility per dollar spent on cassettes or magazines; E = order in which choices are made by consumer.)
   a. Calculate columns B, D, and E for both stereo cassettes and magazines.
   b. What is the equilibrium combination of the two goods for this consumer?
   c. What will happen to the equilibrium if the price of magazines doubles to $1 each?

Table 4-1(a) Stereo Cassettes ($2 each)

A Number Bought	B Money Spent	C MU_s	D MU_s/P_s	E Choice
1	—	60	—	—
2	—	50	—	—
3	—	40	—	—
4	—	30	—	—
5	—	20	—	—
6	—	10	—	—

Table 4-1(b) Magazines (50 cents each)

A Number Bought	B Money Spent	C MU_m	D MU_m/P_m	E Choice
1	—	40	—	—
2	—	30	—	—
3	—	20	—	—
4	—	10	—	—
5	—	0	—	—
6	—	0	—	—

7. Given the two equilibrium combinations of goods in problem 6, draw the consumer's demand curve for magazines. Use Figure 4-1. Why does the consumer's demand curve for magazines have the slope it does?

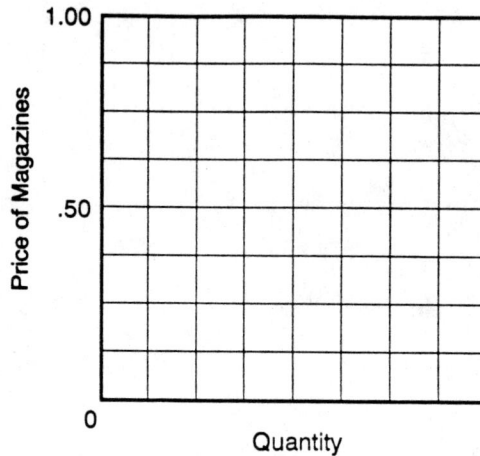

Figure 4-1 Graph for Problem 7

8. You are given the demand schedule shown in Table 4-2.
   a. Calculate the price elasticity of demand between each pair of prices ($5.00 to $4.50, and so on).
   b. What happens to E_d as price falls? Why does this occur?
   c. What factors affect E_d?

Table 4-2 Demand Schedule for Problem 8

Price	Quantity Demanded	E_d
$5.00	2	
4.50	3	
4.00	4	
3.50	5	
3.00	6	
2.50	7	

9. Which principle concerning the marginal utility of income do you accept? Starting from this choice, what do you conclude about the desirability of redistributing income?

10. What factors other than changes in utility do you consider most important in making a normative judgment about whether income should be redistributed?

11. Define and give an example of the application of the concept of income elasticity of demand: of cross price elasticity of demand.

12. State the factors that affect price elasticity of demand. Choose two goods and using these factors discuss what determines their elasticity.

13. Use your understanding of price elasticity of demand to explain the *different* effects on the price of luxury cars compared with cigarettes of the GST. Illustrate with appropriate graphs.

PART 4 Self-test

SECTION A True/false questions

T   F   1. Demand is the quantity of a good or service that consumers buy at a particular price.

T   F   2. Only a change in the price of a good can cause a change in the quantity of it demanded.

T   F   3. The income effect depends on consumers' having more *money* income to spend.

T   F   4. For a given good, the substitution effect comes into force because of a change in the price of another good.

T   F   5. Veblen goods appeal to snobbishness, so consumers buy more of them at high prices than at low prices.

T   F   6. Economists can measure utility.

T   F   7. In analyzing demand, economists usually assume diminishing marginal utility of income.

T   F   8. A perfectly elastic demand curve is one in which the price of a good does not change as the quantity of it demanded changes.

T   F   9. If the demand for a good is unit elastic, quantity demanded does not change as the price of the good changes.

T   F   10. The price elasticity of demand for a good increases with its degree of substitutability for other goods.

T   F   11. Economists usually assume increasing marginal utility of income.

T   F   12. Utility is not the same thing as happiness.

T   F   13. Since 1960, cash income has been substantially redistributed in the United States.

T   F   14. Government transfer payments have had little effect on the distribution of income in the United States.

T   F   15. Economic analysis leads to a unique conclusion about what is the "best" distribution of income.

T   F   16. If price falls, total revenue will increase if the demand for the good is elastic.

T   F   17. If income elasticity of a good is greater than one than that good is an inferior one.

T   F   18. If a good has a large number of substitutes and you can postpone its consumption the demand for the good tends to be elastic.

SECTION B Multiple-choice questions

1. Which one of the following "facts" about consumers do economists *not* assume?
   a. Consumers know their alternatives.
   b. Consumers form expectations about future prices.
   c. Consumers sometimes cannot choose among alternatives.
   d. Consumers seek maximum satisfaction.

2. Which of the following is most likely to be an income-inferior good?
   a. Hamburgers
   b. Color television sets
   c. Skiing trips
   d. Education

3. Which one of the following do economists *not* assume when they are constructing a model of demand?
   a. A consumer can influence the price he or she pays.
   b. Consumers have full information.
   c. Consumers seek maximum utility.
   d. Consumers are rational.

4. Which of the following do economists usually assume?
   a. Constant marginal utility
   b. Increasing marginal utility
   c. Diminishing marginal utility
   d. Diminishing marginal utility beyond some point

5. Which of the following holds true for all points on demand curves?
   a. The marginal utility of each good bought is equated with the marginal utility of each other good.
   b. For each good, marginal utility divided by income is equal.
   c. The marginal utility per dollar spent on each good is equal.
   d. Marginal utility divided by income is irrelevant.

6. Most straight-line demand curves have which characteristic?
   a. Constant elasticity throughout
   b. Elasticities that vary throughout
   c. Unit elasticity throughout
   d. Zero elasticity throughout

7. Which of the following does *not* determine the price elasticity of demand for a good?
   a. Postponability
   b. Price
   c. Proportion of income spent on the good
   d. Length of time involved

8. Which of the following is correct?
   a. Utility and happiness are not necessarily the same.
   b. Utility and happiness are known to be closely related.
   c. Economists assume that utility and happiness are the same.
   d. Economists can measure utility and happiness.

9. Since 1960, the distribution of cash income in the United States has done which one of the following?
   a. Changed in favor of upper-income groups
   b. Changed hardly at all
   c. Changed in favor of lower-income groups
   d. Not been affected by government transfer payments

10. Which of the following is *not* a transfer payment?
    a. Disability payments
    b. Farm subsidies
    c. Purchases of defense goods
    d. Unemployment compensation

11. If demand is elastic and price increases then:
    a. Total revenue will fall
    b. Total revenue will rise
    c. Total revenue will be unchanged
    d. Total revenue may rise or fall

12. Which of the following defines cross price elasticity of demand?
    a. The rate at which quantity demanded changes with a change in price.
    b. The rate at which quantity demanded changes with a change in income.
    c. The rate at which the demand for one good changes as the price of another good changes.
    d. The change in quantity is proportional to a change in price.

SECTION C Matching questions

Match the phrases in column B to the terms in column A.

Column A	*Column B*
1. Income effect	(a) A set of relationships between prices and quantities
2. Marginal utility	(b) Caviar
3. Paradox of value	(c) Result of relative price change
4. Demand	(d) Result of change in purchasing power
5. Transfer payment	(e) Additional satisfaction
6. Law of demand	(f) Diamonds and water
7. Veblen good	(g) Varying elasticities
8. Util	(h) Unemployment compensation
9. Substitution effect	(i) Unit of satisfaction
10. Straight-line demand curve	(j) Price and quantity inversely related

ANSWERS

Part 4

Section A   1, F; 2, T; 3, F; 4, F; 5, T; 6, F; 7, T; 8, T; 9, F; 10, T; 11, F; 12, T; 13, F; 14, F; 15, F; 16, T; 17, F; 18, T

Section B   1, *c*; 2, *a*; 3, *a*; 4, *d*; 5, *c*; 6, *b*; 7, *b*; 8, *a*; 9, *b*; 10, *c*; 11, a; 12, *c*

Section C   1, d; 2, e; 3, f; 4, a; 5, h; 6, j; 7, b; 8, i; 9, c; 10, g

CHAPTER 5   *The Supply Side of the Market*

Application 5   *Markets for Illegal Goods*

PART 1

Reread the sections entitled "Summing Up" at the end of Chapter 5 and Application 5. These give an excellent review of the material in chapter and application.

Things to Watch For

Chapter 5

Chapter 5 deals with **supply**. Supply is the set of relationships between various prices that may exist for a firm's product and the quantities that the firm (or industry) will offer for sale over that range of prices in a given period of time.

A competitive firm is one that cannot influence either the price at which it sells its product or the price it pays for its resources. In other words, that firm is a quantity adjuster. The supply of products it offers for sale is determined by *costs of production.* Costs depend on two things: (1) *prices* of resources, and (2) *productivity* of resources. Since a competitive firm cannot affect prices of its resources, it can influence its costs only by combining resources in their most productive ways. A firm's costs include not only money costs (payments to resources) but also *psychic costs,* or nonmoney costs. The firm's *economic* costs are equal to the prices it pays to resources times the quantities of resources it uses.

Economic costs include both **explicit costs,** those that result from payments to resources contracted for in the market, and **implicit costs,** those associated with using resources the firm itself owns. Full **opportunity costs** of using resources must include both, since resources owned by the firm have alternative uses and could earn factor payments if supplied to the market.

There are various concepts of profit that it is important to understand. Accounting profit is the difference between total revenue and total explicit costs. A normal profit is an implicit cost, an amount just large enough to bid entrepreneurship into producing that good. An economic profit is a return above a normal profit. Finally economic losses occur when returns are less than a normal profit.

Economists distinguish four time periods during which the firm may vary its costs, methods, or output. (1) The **market period** is one in which all output has already been produced. All resources are fixed; none is variable any longer. (2) The **short-run period** is one in which the firm has at least one variable input (usually labor) and therefore can vary its output through variations in the use of that input in conjunction with its fixed input or inputs. (3) The **long-run period** is one in which all resources are variable and the firm can combine them in any way that current technology permits. (Thus, this is a planning period.) (4) The **historical period** is one in which all resources are variable and even technology itself changes. These four periods are useful for analytical purposes. They do not, however, correspond to specific amounts of calendar time, so don't try to associate them with calendar periods.

Firms in the short run or actual production period have two types of costs: **fixed costs**, those *not* associated with changes in output, and **variable costs**, those that *are* associated with changes in output. These costs relate to the time periods as follows.

In the market period, all production costs are fixed costs (payments to inputs for output already produced). Since there are no variable inputs, supply is fixed or perfectly inelastic; it is represented by a vertical "curve" rising from the quantity axis.

In the short run, there are both fixed and variable costs. Total fixed costs, by definition, do not vary. Total variable costs increase as the firm hires additional resources. The rate at which it hires them depends on productivity. A common hypothesis about productivity in the short run is the **law of variable proportions or diminishing returns**. This law states that as a firm uses successive equal units of a variable input in conjunction with a fixed input, the additions to output derived from that variable input begin to diminish beyond some point. The law, which is logically correct but hard to prove statistically, explains what happens to supply in the short run. It also explains what happens to total cost and to **marginal cost**, which is the cost of producing an additional unit of output. According to the law of variable proportions, in the short run marginal productivity will ultimately diminish as the firm uses more of the variable input. When this happens, total cost rises at an increasing rate, since each added unit of resource is paid the same price but is producing less and less. Once a firm feels the effect of diminishing marginal productivity, both its total variable costs and its total costs (the difference between the two being total fixed costs) will increase at a growing rate. This means that its marginal cost rises.

Thus, in the short run, marginal cost which depends on the marginal productivity of the variable resource, ultimately rises. Because of this, the short-run supply curve slopes upward. The firm supplies more only at higher prices. Indeed, the rising marginal-cost curve of the short-run competitive firm is its supply curve. (That is, it is the curve for all prices at which the firm will supply anything to the market.)

Long-run supply depends entirely on variable costs, since in the long run all costs are variable. In the long run, firms can choose different plant sizes. Total cost (total variable cost) may do one of three things. (1) Total cost may grow at a diminishing rate. Larger plant sizes may lead to increased efficiency. As this happens, average cost (TC/output) will decrease as marginal cost falls. This situation is referred to as **economies of scale**. (2) Total cost may grow at a constant rate. Each plant size may be just as efficient as each other plant size. When this happens, both average cost and marginal cost are constant. This situation is referred to as *constant returns to scale*. (3) Total cost may grow at an increasing rate. Larger plant sizes may turn out to be less efficient. Then average and marginal costs rise. Economists refer to this as **diseconomies of scale**.

Economies of scale arise from (1) specialization and division of labor, (2) improved management, (3) complete utilization of processes, and (4) more efficient plant and equipment. Diseconomies of scale arise from **discommunication**, or failure to communicate effectively in large organizations.

One obtains a figure for supply of goods by an entire industry, like demand by a market, by adding the quantities supplied by each firm at each price for the good (*aggregation*). As long as the economies of scale are all **internal economies of scale** (internal to firms), the addition is simple. One adds all the quantities supplied by each firm at each price. If the various firms' economies of scale are **external economies of scale**—that is, if they are brought about by variations in output of the entire industry—then the adding process is more complex.

One often wants to know the *elasticity of supply,* which is the rate at which quantity supplied changes as price changes. The formula for calculating the elasticity of supply (E_s) is

$$E_s = \frac{\Delta Q/Q}{\Delta P/P} = \frac{\text{change in quantity/quantity}}{\text{change in price/price}}$$

$$= \frac{[Q_2 - Q_1]/[(Q_1 + Q_2)/2]}{[P_2 - P_1]/[(P_1 + P_2)/2]} = \frac{(Q_2 - Q_1)/(Q_1 + Q_2)}{(P_2 - P_1)/(P_1 + P_2)}.$$

This is the average rate of change. Elasticity of supply E_s may be (1) *elastic,* in which case the quantity supplied changes at a faster rate than price, (2) *inelastic,* in which case the quantity supplied changes at a slower rate than price, or (3) *unit elastic,* in which case the quantity supplied changes at the same rate as price.

Time is the most important factor affecting the elasticity of supply. As the time available for improving technology and using different combinations of resources grows, so does E_s. In the very long run (the historical period), technological change also becomes a very important influence on E_s.

Finally, remember that supply is relatively easy to identify for a competitive firm or industry. When we leave competition and deal with other kinds of markets, however, firms become interdependent in their responses to price changes, and it becomes very difficult to identify supply. Instead, economists concentrate on costs.

Application 5

To sell illegal goods is to commit economic crimes. Apart from the moral and other aspects of such actions, there are economic effects as well. For example, sales of illegal goods are not calculated in the GNP.

The first nationwide effort to make certain goods illegal was prohibition. In the 1920s, the United States voted in the Eighteenth Amendment to the Constitution, which made the manufacture, possession, or sale of alcoholic beverages illegal. The economic effects of this were that supply fell, prices rose, and illegal markets developed. It took another amendment to the Constitution to repeal this one.

What happens if the sale of an illegal good becomes legal? Suppose the sale of cocaine is made legal. (1) Supply, determined by the costs of the seller, should increase. (2) Costs of risk would fall. (3) Costs of information would be reduced (because of availability of different brands, plus economies of scale in mass communication). (4) Larger firms, such as the legitimate drug industry, would enter the picture. In short, there should be a significant increase in supply. As for demand: (1) Judging from some studies of cocaine use, the price elasticity of demand is fairly small. (2) The income elasticity of demand for cocaine is an unknown factor.

A large increase in the (legal) supply of cocaine, plus a small price elasticity of demand (most of the change in demand would apparently be on the part of older people) would result in a fairly small increase in the consumption, or quantity demanded. *Note:*

That is not necessarily a compelling argument in favor of legalization. Legal, moral, and medical aspects must be considered as well.

The student should also understand the effects of present drug enforcement policy which attempts to reduce supply through strict enforcement, as well as the alternative of reverse price discrimination (offering lower prices to addicts along with higher prices to dabblers) in order to understand the effects of legalizing drugs and finally the effects of policy options that confront the nation today.

PART 2

Define the following terms and concepts.

1. Supply
2. Quantity adjuster
3. Opportunity costs
4. Economic costs
5. Explicit costs
6. Implicit costs
7. Accounting Profit
8. Normal profit
9. Economic profit
10. Market period
11. Short run
12. Long run
13. Historical period
14. Variable costs
15. Fixed costs
16. Law of variable proportions or marginal product
17. Marginal cost
18. Economies of scale
19. Diseconomies of scale
20. Constant returns to scale
21. Diseconomies
22. Internal economies of scale
23. External economies of scale
24. Pure elasticity of supply
25. Reverse price discrimination

PART 3

Answer the following questions and problems.

1. Why must firms that do not include (and cover) both their explicit and implicit costs of production be operating inefficiently?

2. Have any psychic costs influenced you in your choice of career or job? Discuss.

3. Evaluate the following statement: "*Normal profit* is necessary in order to assure that resources are being used in the most efficient way."

4. How would a business person use the various concepts of profits in business planning?

5. What are the factors that affect supply in the market period? the short-run period? the long-run period? the historical period?

6. Provide a numerical example of the typical behaviour of marginal product using labour as your variable factor of production. Assume a wage rate of $12 per hour to derive the implicit marginal cost data. Graph your marginal product and marginal cost curves.

7. Consider Figure 5-1, and then do the following things.
   a. For a given competitive firm, draw (1) the short-run average-fixed-cost curve, (2) the short-run average-variable-cost curve, (3) the short-run average-total-cost curve, and (4) the short-run marginal-cost curve.
   b. Explain why marginal cost must equal average variable cost and average total cost when they are at their lowest points.
   c. Explain the relationship between this competitive firm's marginal cost and its supply.

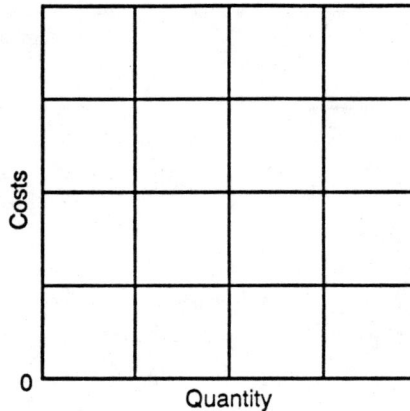

Figure 5-1 Short-Run Costs

8. Using Figure 5-2, draw the supply curve for a given firm in its market period and its short-run period.

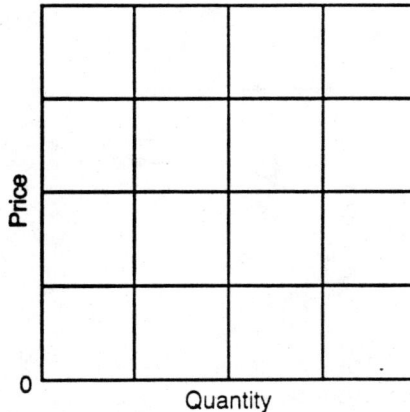

Figure 5-2 Supply Curves: Market and Short-Run Periods

9. Use Figure 5-3 to depict the following things for a given firm.
   a. Draw a long-run average-cost curve that reflects economies of scale, constant returns to scale, and diseconomies of scale at different rates of output.
   b. Why is the curve you have drawn called an envelope curve?

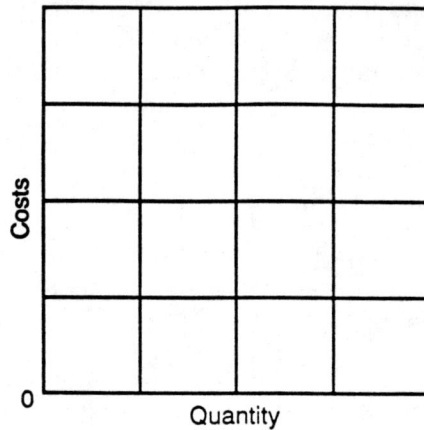

Figure 5-3 Long-Run Costs

10. Use Figure 5-4 to do the following things.
    a. Draw long-run supply curves for a firm that is experiencing (1) economies of scale, (2) diseconomies of scale, and (3) constant returns to scale.
    b. Suggest what may happen to the supply of this firm in the historical period.

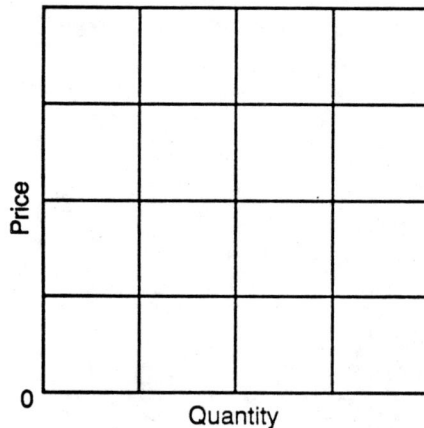

Figure 5-4 Long-Run Supply

11. What is the major problem in identifying the supply curves of firms in noncompetitive industries?

12. What factors are most influential in determining the elasticity of supply?

13. When a legal good is made illegal, or an illegal good is made legal, what factors determine the effects on demand, supply, and price?

14. Use your understanding of price elasticity of supply to explain the *different* effects of the GST on the equilibrium price of agricultural products compared with manufactured products. Illustrate with appropriate graphs.

PART 4 Self-test

SECTION A True/false questions

T	F	1.	A firm's costs of production are determined by prices of resources and productivity of resources.
T	F	2.	A normal profit is what is left over after paying resources and is not, therefore, a cost of production.
T	F	3.	In the market period a firm can increase output fairly easily.
T	F	4.	Supply depends heavily on the amount of time firms have to respond to changes in the market.
T	F	5.	Accounting profits is the same as normal profits.
T	F	6.	In the long run all costs of production are fixed costs.
T	F	7.	In the market period the supply curve of a firm is perfectly inelastic.
T	F	8.	The law of variable proportions applies only to the short run.
T	F	9.	Average fixed cost always decreases as output increases.
T	F	10.	Economies of scale are associated with the short run.
T	F	11.	Constant returns to scale are the same as constant long-run average costs.
T	F	12.	Illegal goods are not included in calculations of the GNP.
T	F	13.	Legalizing a good is likely to decrease its supply.
T	F	14.	Legalizing goods reduces information costs.
T	F	15.	The price of a good is likely to increase if that good is made illegal.
T	F	16.	The price elasticity of demand for cocaine is likely to be small.
T	F	17.	Under no circumstance would reverse price discrimination be an acceptable option in terms of drug control policy.

SECTION B Multiple-choice questions

1. Supply is fixed (perfectly inelastic) in which one of the following periods?
    a. Short run
    b. Market
    c. Long run
    d. Historical

2. Supply is likely to be most elastic in which period?
   a. Long run
   b. Market
   c. Short run
   d. Historical

3. Which of the following is most correct about normal profit?
   a. Just large enough to bid entreprenural talent into producing that product.
   b. Implicit cost
   c. Equal to accounting profit
   d. *a* & *b* are both correct

4. The input most likely to be variable for a firm is
   a. Land.
   b. Labor.
   c. Capital.
   d. Entrepreneurship

5. Which one of the following is *not* likely to be a fixed cost?
   a. Interest payments
   b. Wages
   c. Insurance
   d. Mortgage payments

6. For a competitive firm, short-run supply is the same as
   a. average fixed cost.
   b. average variable cost.
   c. average total cost.
   d. marginal cost.

7. Diseconomies of scale are likely to result from which one of the following?
   a. Inefficient use of capital
   b. Rising fixed costs
   c. Increasing wages
   d. Discommunication

8. External economies of scale are caused by which one of the following?
   a. Efficient organization of the firm
   b. More efficient organization of the firm's plant
   c. Changes in industry output
   d. Better firm management

9. Elastic supply means that
   a. $\Delta Q/Q = \Delta P/P$.
   b. $\Delta Q/Q < \Delta P/P$.
   c. $\Delta Q/Q > \Delta P/P$.
   d. $\Delta Q/Q + \Delta P/P = 1$.

10. Prohibition of alcohol sales in the United States led to which one of the following?
    a. Increased supply
    b. Better quality control
    c. Lower prices
    d. Higher prices

11. Which one of the following is a likely result of legalizing an illegal good?
    a. Lower costs of risk
    b. Higher information costs
    c. Black markets
    d. Diseconomies of scale

12. The policy option of reverse price discrimination in regard to legalizing cocaine:
    a. Would charge a lower price to addicts in an effort to reduce crime.
    b. Would never be done because quantity demanded of cocaine would decline.
    c. Would charge a higher price to addicts to discourage consumption.
    d. Would subsidize the seller of cocaine.

SECTION C Matching questions

Match the phrases in column B to the terms in column A.

Column A	*Column B*
1. Normal profit	(a) Decreased by legalization
2. Economic profit	(b) Schedule of price-quantity relationships
3. Market period	(c) Self-owned capital
4. Information costs	(d) Entrepreneur's opportunity cost
5. Historical period	(e) Inelastic supply
6. Diminishing returns	(f) Not a cost of production
7. Supply	(g) Input that is likely to be variable in the short run
8. Discommunication	(h) Change in technology
9. Implicit costs	(i) Variable proportions
10. Labor	(j) Diseconomies of scale
11. Reverse price discrimination	(k) High price to dabblers, low price to addicts

ANSWERS

Part 4

Section A 1,T; 2,F; 3,F; 4,T; 5, F; 6,F; 7,T; 8,T; 9,T; 10,F; 11,T; 12,T; 13,F; 14,T; 15,T; 16,T; 17, F
Section B 1, *b;* 2, *d;* 3, *d;* 4, *b,;* 5, *b;* 6, *d;* 7, *d;* 8, *c;* 9, *c;* 10, *d;* 11, *a;* *12, a;*
Section C 1, d; 2, f; 3, e; 4, a; 5, h; 6, i; 7, b; 8, j; 9, c; 10, g; 11, k

CHAPTER 6   *Market Equilibrium: Do Private Markets Always Produce What is Socially Desirable?*

Application 6   *How Much Clean Air Do We Want to Buy?*

PART 1

Reread the sections entitled "Summing Up" at the end of Chapter 6 and Application 6. They provide an excellent review of the material in chapter and application.

Things to Watch For

Chapter 6

This chapter is about two closely related subjects: (1) equilibrium pricing and output, and (2) possible divergences between *private* and *public* equilibrium pricing and output.

The **equilibrium price** is a price established by the independent influences of supply and demand. The word *equilibrium,* as used by economists, means the central tendency of a thing or things. The equilibrium condition for prices is that quantity supplied should equal quantity demanded. Any price *above* the equilibrium price leads to excess supply. Any price *below* the equilibrium price leads to excess demand. Thus, the equilibrium price is the price that does away with excess demand and supply. It is the price at which quantity demanded is equal to quantity supplied.

The amounts of goods and services that firms supply to the market are based on firms' assessment of their own private costs and benefits. Sometimes, these private costs and benefits and **social costs** (the opportunity cost to society of using up certain resources) and benefits are not the same. Differences between private costs and benefits and social ones are called **externalities** or **spillovers**. Social costs are the sum of private costs plus spillovers. (If there are no spillovers, private and social costs are the same.)

Spillovers exist when privately produced goods (steel, chemicals, automobiles, and so on) are not fully costed by the industries that make them. Such industries, when they are assessing the costs of their products, fail to take into account the hidden costs of cleaning up the air and water they pollute. This means that they set the price of their product too low. As a result, the public consumes too much steel, too many cars, too many of all of these underpriced goods. In effect, society is allocating too many of its scarce resources to the production of these commodities. These are not private costs, but public ones. Can they be **internalized**? That is, can the public cause private producers and consumers to assume the burden of these social costs? Economists say yes, both for cost externalities and for benefit externalities; they cite industries' efforts at conservation, and some educational activities undertaken by industrial producers. (Application 6 takes up this subject as it relates to clean air.)

Chapter 6 discusses the question of whether government action to force industry to internalize spillovers would destroy property rights. If the government forced producers to include spillovers, it would definitely abridge some private property rights. But these rights are not absolutes. Any society must try to strike a balance between private rights and social rights. Some internalization of benefits and costs can occur even under a free-market system. That is, people who receive benefits compensate the people who have lost property rights through having had to internalize certain costs.

If government does intervene where spillovers exist, it should be up to the point at which the **marginal social cost** of intervening is equal to the **marginal social benefit** of incorporating the externality. In other words, if industries take the externality into account when they are making decisions about production, and if the public takes it into account when making decisions about consumption, the marginal social cost should equal the marginal social benefit.

A qualification for a market economy lies in the use of resource held in common. These common property resources are open to use by everyone. They have no individual owners. An important problem that we meet again in the text is the **"free rider problem"**. This is that once public goods are produced, they are available to everyone even those that had not contributed to the cost of producing them.

Application 6

Application 6 discusses the controversies between economists and ecologists over solutions to problems of environmental pollution. Some ecologists have made horrifying predictions of ecological disasters that they say will come to pass as early as the end of this decade. Others predict depletion of vital resources plus mass starvation by the end of this century. (The Club of Rome study and the books of Paul Ehrlich are examples.) Economists are wary of these dire projections because (1) the doomsday forecasters base their argument on linear projections (the idea that present trends will continue) in resource usage and population growth, and (2) they imply that government and industry act in collusion, and that a system of private free markets fails to offer even a partial solution.

Economists do not lay claim to having any quick, easy solutions to environmental problems. However, they do realize certain things: (1) The problems are economic in origin. To explain environmental problems, economists often rely on the **materials-balance approach,** the relation of the input that is used to produce goods to the waste products that must be disposed of when the goods are consumed. (2) Environmental pollution has caused things such as clean air, which used to be considered a free good (one with zero price), to become scarce commodities, commodities with opportunity costs. (3) Because of population growth, economic growth, lack of incentives to avoid pollution, and technological change, clean air and water must now have a price attached to them. Many economists believe that the pricing process will require government intervention.

Studies by economists have shown that clean air (or water) *can* be priced. One can establish the demand for it by sampling or balloting. The results so far indicate a downward-sloping demand curve. In other words, at lower prices, people are willing to buy more. The supply curve for clean air slopes upward because of rising marginal cost. The costs of achieving clean air—the costs of financing the equilibrium amount of clean air—can be met by (1) imposing special taxes on polluters, or (2) selling "rights" to pollute up to a point determined by the market demand for clean air. The rising price of these rights would ultimately provide industry with the incentive to install antipollution equipment in its factories and—at least in the important case of cars—in its products.

Some people (economists among them) feel that the questions involved in such a market process are too technical for consumers to deal with. They believe that it would be better if the government imposed standards that forced firms and consumers to internalize the costs of "producing" the equilibrium amount of clean air, rather than letting the market bring about this result.

Still other people feel that neither of these approaches—market nor government— is adequate, because both ignore or understate the esthetic value of clean air and water. Many economists feel that the consuming public (or its elected representatives) ought to set the standards, even the esthetic ones. If neither the public nor the governing bodies do so, who will?

PART 2

Define the following terms and concepts.

1. Competitive market conditions
2. Private equilibrium
3. Marginal private cost or benefit
4. Marginal social cost or benefit
5. Externalities (spillovers)
6. Social (public) costs
7. Internalizing
8. Public equilibrium
9. Private and public property rights
10. Public goods
11. Free rider problem
12. Linear extrapolation
13. Materials-balance approach

PART 3

Answer the following questions and problems.

1. Evaluate the following statement: "The beauty of a competitive market is that it always results in a price and a rate of output that are socially desirable."

2. Look at Figure 6-1 and answer the following questions.
   a. Which is equilibrium price?
   b. Which is equilibrium output?
   c. What does the distance AB measure?
   d. What does the distance CD measure?
   e. What factors cause the equilibrium price to tend to be established?

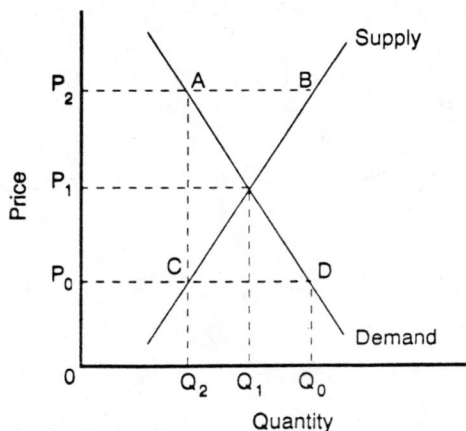

Figure 6-1 Equilibrium Price

3. Evaluate the statement, "Public (social) costs are never the same as private costs."

4. Look at Figure 6-2 and answer the following questions.
   a. What does the distance RS measure
   b. What is the private equilibrium output?
   c. What is the public equilibrium output?
   d. What does demand represent in terms of benefits to private consumers? to the public?
   e. What means exist to make the public and the private equilibrium the same?

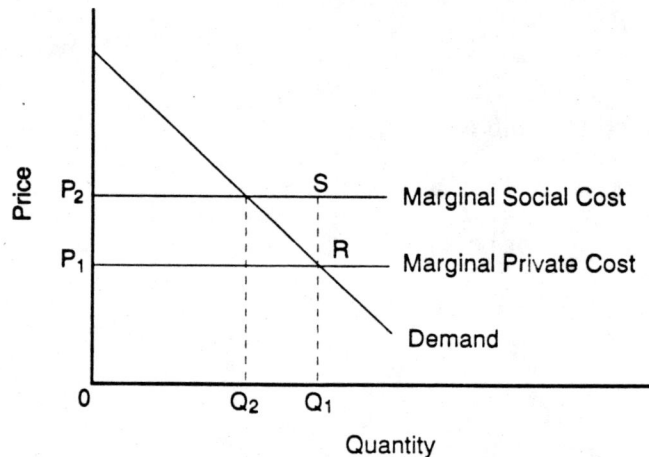

Figure 6-2 Private and Public Equilibrium

5. How do common property resources and public goods affect market decisions and decisions about output? What does the free rider problem have to do with these decisions?

6. As a society moves to provide cleaner air and water, will it have to abridge existing property rights? Why or why not?

7. What are public goods? Are there instances in which these goods can be provided by private firms? If so, under what circumstances?

8. What is the basis of the belief of many economists that private markets can help solve many environmental-pollution problems?

9. Upon what basis do many ecologists conclude that market solutions to environmental problems are impossible or prohibitively expensive?

PART 4 Self-test

SECTION A True/false questions

T F 1. When the price of a commodity is above the equilibrium point, excess supply results.

T F 2. When the price of a commodity is below equilibrium, excess demand results.

T F 3. When marginal social cost and marginal private cost are not the same, spillovers result.

T F 4. Economists in general believe that government must intervene in each instance of spillover.

T F 5. It is impossible for the government or the public to cause private firms and consumers to internalize externalities.

T F 6. Some economists regard special taxes and the selling of "rights" to pollute as appropriate means of dealing with spillovers.

T F 7. Internalizing externalities always means destroying private property rights.

T F 8. When government intervenes in cases in which there are spillovers, it should take action up to the point at which marginal social cost equals marginal social benefit.

T F 9. According to some ecologists, the free market offers no solutions to environmental problems.

T F 10. Common property resources are privately owned but publically controlled.

T F 11. The free rider problem involves people having acess to public goods but not contributing to the cost of producing them.

T F 12. The materials-balance approach involves a relationship between output (GNP) and waste disposal.

T F 13. One can establish a community's demand for clean air by sampling or by allowing the citizenry to vote.

T F 14. The curve depicting the supply of clean air slopes down to the right.

T F 15. There are people who are not satisfied by either market-determined or government-imposed standards for clean air and water.

SECTION B Multiple-choice questions

1. An equilibrium price does all but which of the following?
   a. Equates quantity supplied with quantity demanded
   b. Eliminates excess demand
   c. Makes the supply curve and the demand curve equal
   d. Eliminates excess supply

2. Which statement about gasoline prices is *not* correct?
   a. Gasoline prices cause the users of gasoline to internalize all externalities.
   b. Gasoline prices fail to cause the users of gasoline to internalize externalities.
   c. Gasoline prices are such that private and social costs are equal.
   d. Gasoline prices are such that private and social benefits are equal.

3. Which statement about private and public (social) equilibrium rates of consumption is *not* correct?
   a. The two rates are always the same.
   b. The two rates may diverge.
   c. The two rates may be the same.
   d. The two rates always have some relationship to each other.

4. Which one of the following is not considered a benefit externality?
   a. Public parks
   b. Shade trees
   c. Public libraries
   d. Single-occupant automobiles

5. Government intervention in cases of spillover should continue up to the point at which
   a. marginal social benefit equals marginal social cost
   b. marginal social cost equals average social cost
   c. marginal social benefit equals average social cost.
   d. total social benefit equals total social cost.

6. Which of the following is not classified as a public good?
   a. Nuclear aircraft carriers
   b. Radio signals
   c. B-1 bombers
   d. Steel mills

7. The best example from the following of a common property resource is:
   a. cadillac owned by Edna Brown.
   b. A micro-chip factory owned by ITT.
   c. Grand Canyon National Park operated by the National Park Service.
   d. A Toyota import owned by Nissan Corporation.

8. The "free rider problem" concerns some economists because:
   a. More people can ride on an airplane when not used to capacity.
   b. People who don't pay any costs can use public goods.
   c. The homeless do not pay taxes.
   d. Some of the rich able to employ tax consultants pay no taxes.

9. When a society sets out to improve the quality of its air, equating the marginal social costs and benefits with the marginal private costs and benefits is likely to result in which one of the following?
   a. Completely clean air
   b. Crisis air pollution
   c. Air quality that is somewhere in between crisis pollution and really clean air
   d. Insoluble problems, since social costs and benefits can't be established

10. Ecologists generally accept all but which one of the following statements?
   a. Nature places limits on growth.
   b. There are absolute limits to growth.
   c. Markets can provide solutions to the problems of pollution.
   d. Our present rates of resource use and population growth will bring about ecological disasters.

11. Economists generally accept all but which one of the following statements?
   a. Environmental problems have economic origins.
   b. It is possible to put a price on the purification of air and water.
   c. Markets can provide solutions to problems related to the environment.
   d. Our present rates of population growth and resource use are bound to continue.

SECTION C Matching questions

Match the phrases in column B to the terms in column A.

Column A	Column B
1. Spillovers	(a) Price below equilibrium
2. Public good	(b) Price above equilibrium
3. Limit of government intervention	(c) Quantity supplied = quantity demanded
4. Equilibrium price	(d) Marginal social cost different from marginal private cost
5. Private goods	(e) Indivisible in use
6. Materials-balance approach	(f) Marginal social cost = marginal social benefit
7. Excess supply	(g) Individuals can be excluded from using them
8. Scarce good	(h) Input of raw materials and output of wastes
9. Free good	(i) Price above zero
10. Excess demand	(j) Price equals zero

ANSWERS

Part 4

Section A 1, T; 2, T; 3, T; 4, F; 5, F; 6, T; 7, F; 8, T; 9, T; 10, F; 11,T; 12, F; 13, T; 14, F; 15, T

Section B 1, *c*; 2, *a*; 3, *a*; 4, *d*; 5, *a*; 6, *d*; 7,*c*; 8, *b*; 9, *c*; 10, *c*; 11, *d*

Section C 1, d; 2, e; 3, f; 4, c; 5, g; 6, h; 7, b; 8, i; 9, j; 10, a

CHAPTER 7   *Pure Competition: One Extreme*

PART 1

Reread the section entitled "Summing Up" at the end for an excellent review of the chapter.

Things to Watch For

Chapter 7

Chapter 7 continues the analysis of the theory of costs developed in Chapter 6, adding in revenues. Then it shows how firms compute profits and analyzes the behavior of individual firms with respect to profits, losses, prices, and output. Chapter 7 also studies the behavior of the firm under conditions that are called purely competitive. The three succeeding chapters deal with firms in other market classifications.

    First the chapter offers a definition of **pure competition**, which is characterized by (1) *many firms*, (2) **homogeneous product**, and (3) *freedom of entry*. These characteristics explain why a single firm in a purely competitive market cannot influence the price of the product. It is the market that determines price. Regardless of its output, the firm must sell at that market-determined price. The purely competitive firm in order to have a basis for its profit maximizing output decision must conjecture about its demand curve. Because the firm is too small to influence price and that it is a price taker (must charge the going market price) then P, AR, and MR being the same, the firm's conjectural demand curve is perfectly elastic.

    The chapter next uses both a total-cost, total-revenue approach and a marginal-cost, marginal-revenue approach for a firm in a short-run situation (the latter is the usual approach). *Note:* A purely competitive firm will maximize profits or minimize losses at the level of output at which its marginal cost equals its marginal revenue.

    In the short run, the purely competitive firm encounters four possible situations. (1) When its prices are greater than its average total costs, it earns an **economic profit**. (Note that the economic profit is possible in the short run only; however, a purely competitive firm could not enter an industry, build a plant, and start operations in a short-run period.) (2) When its prices are just equal to its average total cost, it earns a **normal profit**. Output at a normal profit is also called the break even point. Here all resources, including the entreprenuer, is receiving returns just equal to their contribution to output. (3) When its price is lower than its average total cost but higher than its average variable cost, it sustains an **economic loss with production**. If it shuts down, it must continue to pay all fixed costs, which are greater than its losses; so it *continues to operate at a loss*. (4) When its price is less than its average variable cost, it sustains an **economic loss shutdown**. When this happens, it *ceases operations*. The point where price is equal to average variable costs is called the shut down point. The firm loses as much by producing as it would by shutting down (total fixed costs).

When all four situations are combined into one diagram, a student will see that output at each price (MC equal to demand or price) will occur as long as MC (or price) is above AVC. When they are equal the firm shuts down. Therefore, it is easy to see that the purely competitive firm's short run supply curve is its MC curve above AVC.

In the long run, the purely competitive firm encounters only one situation: normal profits. In a **constant-cost industry**, more and more firms enter the industry, which causes the supply of the product to increase. This leads to a decrease in the price the product will fetch in the marketplace. The falling price eliminates the economic profits that firms in the industry had previously enjoyed. To avoid an economic loss, firms leave the industry. This decreases the supply of the product and causes the price of it to rise again. In an **increasing-cost industry**, if more and more firms enter the industry, costs to the individual firm rise. But if more and more firms leave the industry, costs to the individual firm fall. In an increasing-cost industry, changes in price and cost both lead to a normal profit situation. In a **decreasing-cost industry**, by contrast, as firms enter the industry both price and cost fall.

The main advantage of the purely competitive market is that purely competitive firms achieve the most efficient allocations of resources to produce that combination of goods and services that consumers want. They are able to do so because marginal cost equals price.

Keep in mind that productive efficiency is simply producing at the lowest level of cost. Allocative efficiency is when the economy is producing that combination of goods consumers prefer. Both conditions exist in long run equilibrium under pure competition.

Again, to emphasize the welfare implications of pure competition, the chapter introduces the concepts of consumers' and producers' surplus. The consumers' surplus is the difference between what consumers are willing to pay and what consumers must pay. The producers' surplus, on the other hand, is the difference between the price producers are willing to sell the product for and the market determined price. Under long run equilibrium in a purely competitve market, the sum of consumers' and producers' surpluses is maximized.

The main disadvantage of the purely competitive market is that the output of purely competitive firms tends to lack variety, due to the homogeneity of their product. There are also problems involving use of technology, economies of scale, and rate of growth of technology.

The most important justification for using the purely competitive market as a model is that it provides the ideal with which one can compare the other market situations.

PART 2

Define the following terms and concepts.

1. Pure competition
2. Pure monopoly
3. Imperfect competition
4. Homogeneous products
5. Price taker
6. Price seeker
7. Profit maximization rule
8. Quantity adjuster
9. Shutdown point
10. External economy & diseconomy
11. Normal profit
12. Break even point
13. Increasing-cost industry
14. Decreasing-cost industry
15. Constant-cost industry
16. Economic capacity
17. Allocative efficiency
18. Technical efficiency
19. Consumers' surplus
20. producers' surplus

PART 3

Answer the following questions and problems.

1. Describe the basic characteristics of a purely competitive industry. Give three examples of industries that come close to pure competition. Describe them in terms of the basic characteristics of pure competition.

2. Why does a firm in a purely competitive market charge the same price as the market equilibrium price for the industry, no matter how much the firm produces?

3. In Figure 7-1; draw the relevant curves for the four possible situations a purely competitive firm faces in the short run, using the total-revenue, total-cost approach. Explain each situation. If you have any difficulties, check yourself against Figure 7-1 in the text.

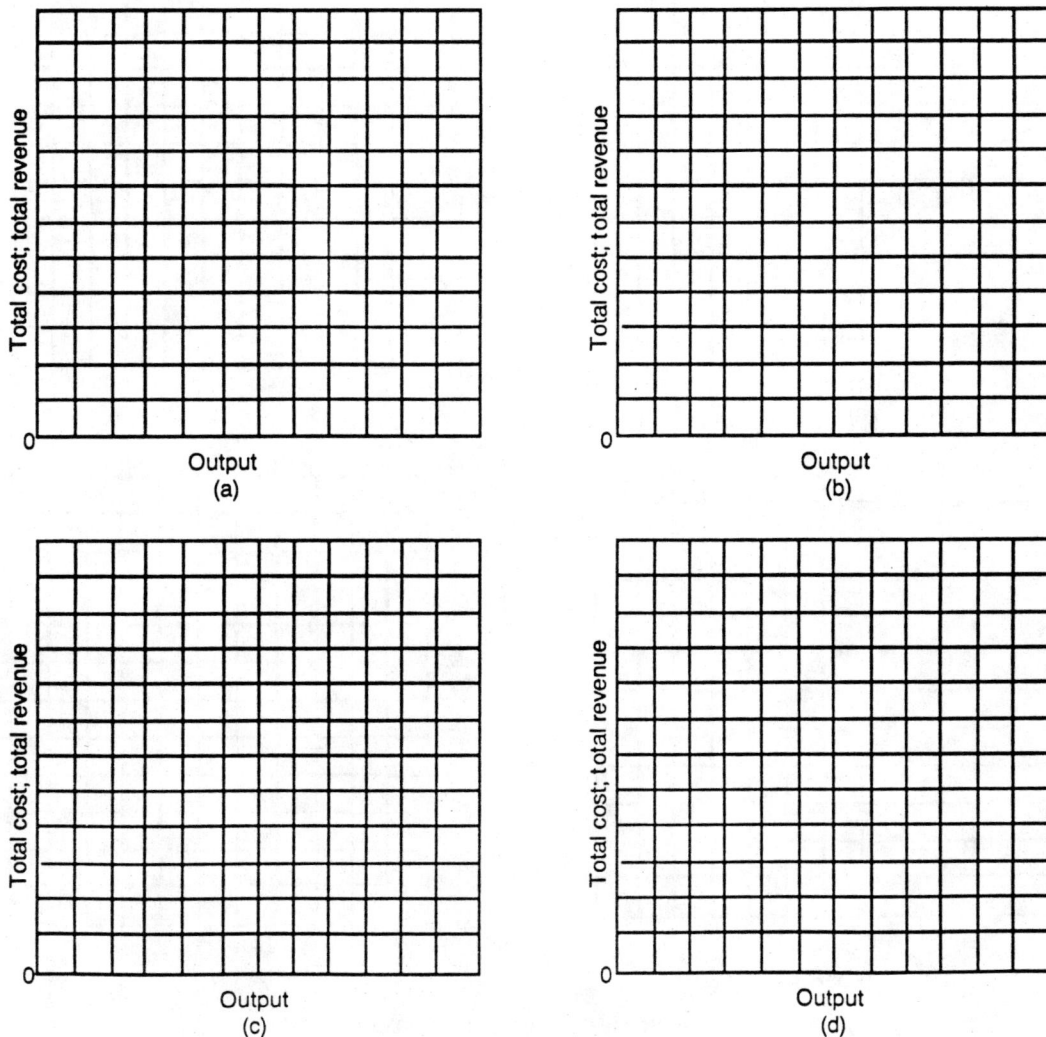

Figure 7-1 Graphs for Problem 3

4. At what level of output would a firm's profits be maximized or its losses minimized? Why?

5. Why is the conjectural demand curve for the purely competitive firm perfectly elastic (a horizontal line)? Why are its demand, average-revenue, and marginal-revenue curves all the same?

6. In Figure 7-2, draw the relevant curves for the four possible profit or loss situations a purely competitive firm faces in the short run, using the marginal-revenue, marginal-cost approach. Explain each situation. Indicate the break even point. The shutdown point. If you have any difficulties, check yourself against Figures 7-3, 7-4, 7-5, and 7-6 in the text.

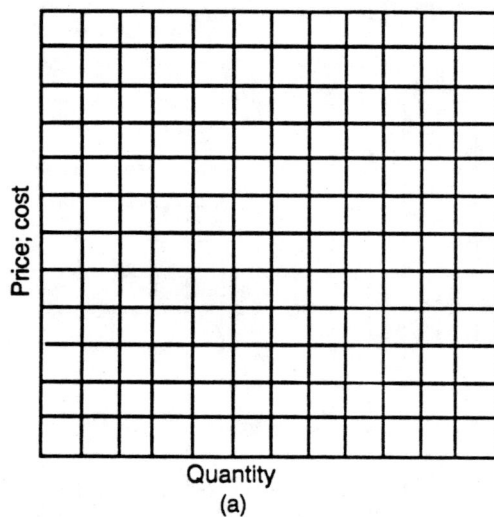

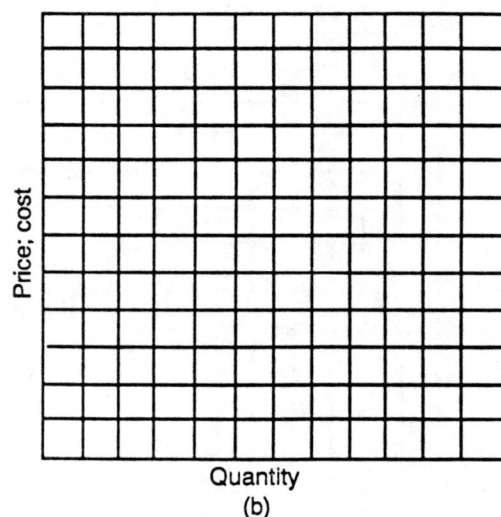

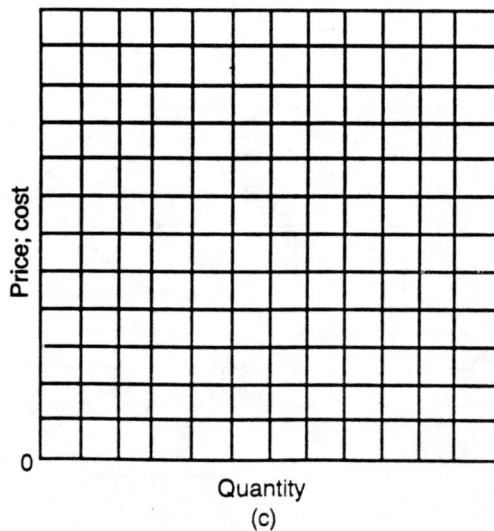

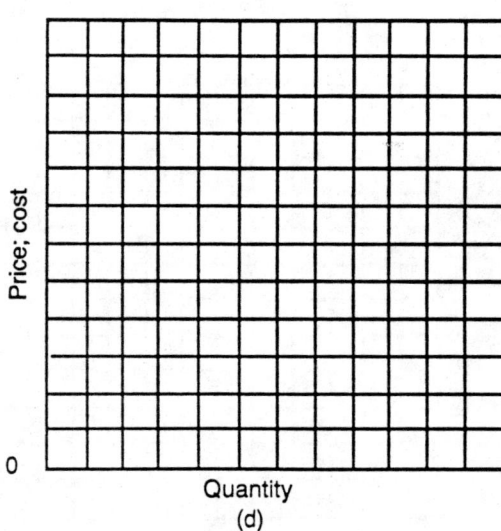

Quantity
(a)

Quantity
(b)

Quantity
(c)

Quantity
(d)

Figure 7-2 Graphs for Problem 6

7. Why is it possible for a purely competitive firm to maintain an economic profit in the short run? Why might it suffer an economic loss? Under what loss conditions would a firm shut down in the short run?

8. Using Figure 7-3, answer the following questions about a purely competitive firm in the short run. (The answers are given after Part 4. If you make any errors, check question 6 to be sure that you understand it completely.)
   a. In situation 1, the relevant demand curve for a firm receiving economic profits is D ____ = AR ____ = MR ____ at price ____. Output that would maximize profits or minimize losses is ____. Economic profits are represented by the rectangle ____.
   b. In situation 2, the relevant demand curve for a firm receiving only a normal profit is D ____ = AR ____ = MR ____ at price ____. Output that would maximize profits is ____. Total cost is rectangle ____. Total revenues are rectangle ____.
   c. In situation 3, the relevant demand curve for a firm incurring economic losses but continuing to produce in the short run is D ____ = AR ____ = MR ____ at price ____. Output that would minimize losses is ____. Economic losses are represented by the rectangle ____. Total fixed costs are represented by the rectangle ____. Economic losses are (*greater than/less than*) total fixed costs. Production (*would/would not*) take place in the short run.
   d. In situation 4, the relevant demand curve for a firm incurring economic losses so large that it shuts down in the short run is D ____ = AR ____ = MR ____. Total fixed costs are represented by the rectangle ____. If production took place, price would be ____ and output ____. Economic losses would be rectangle ____. Total fixed costs would be (*larger than/less than*) economic losses. Production (*would/would not*) take place in the short run.

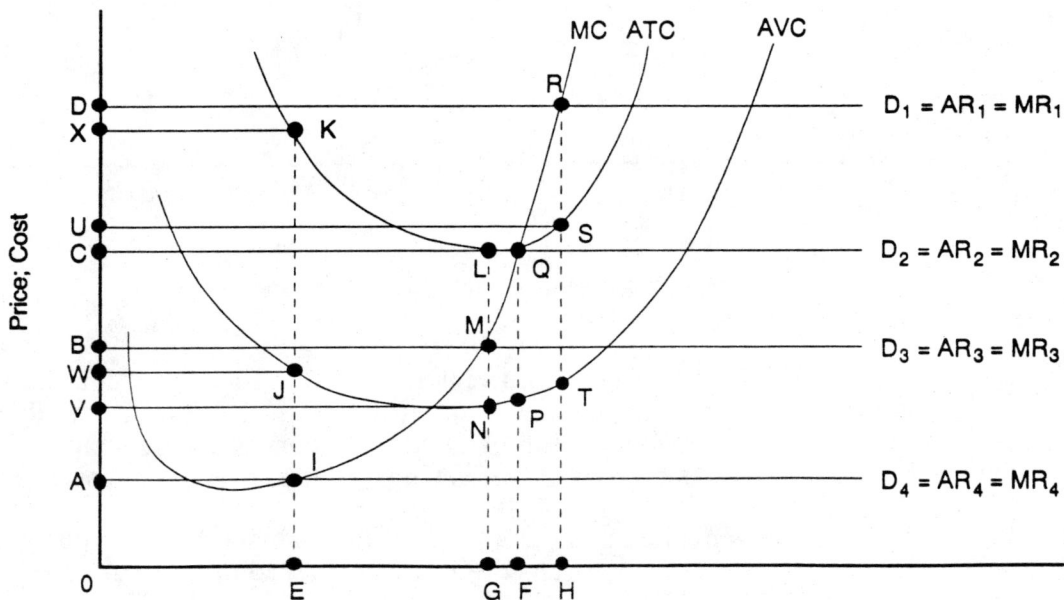

Figure 7-3 Graph for Problems 8 and 9

9. What is the short-run supply curve for the purely competitive firm? Why? You can use Figure 7-3 to help explain why.

10. Figure 7-4(a) shows demand and cost curves for a purely competitive firm in the long run. Figure 7-4 (b) shows demand and supply curves for the entire industry. Use the figure to answer the following questions. (The answers are given after Part 4.)

    a. Suppose that the competitive firm had experienced economic losses in the short run. Its relevant demand curve would be D _____ = AR _____ = MR _____. The supply curve for the industry would be S_____. Price would be _____. What mechanism would work to eliminate the firm's losses in the long run? In the process the $D_1 = AR_1 = MR_1$ curve would shift (*up/down*) and the market supply would (*increase/decrease*).

    b. Suppose that the competitive firm had experienced economic profits in the short run. Its relevant demand curve would be D _____ = AR _____ = MR _____. The supply curve for the industry would be S_____. Price would be _____. What mechanism would work to eliminate the firm's economic profits in the long run? In the process $D_3 = AR_3 = MR_3$ would shift (*up/down*) and the market supply would (*increase/decrease*).

    c. The firm's long run equilibrium curve would be D _____ = AR _____ = MR _____, and for the industry the supply curve would be S_____ at price _____. Why would that be the only possibility?

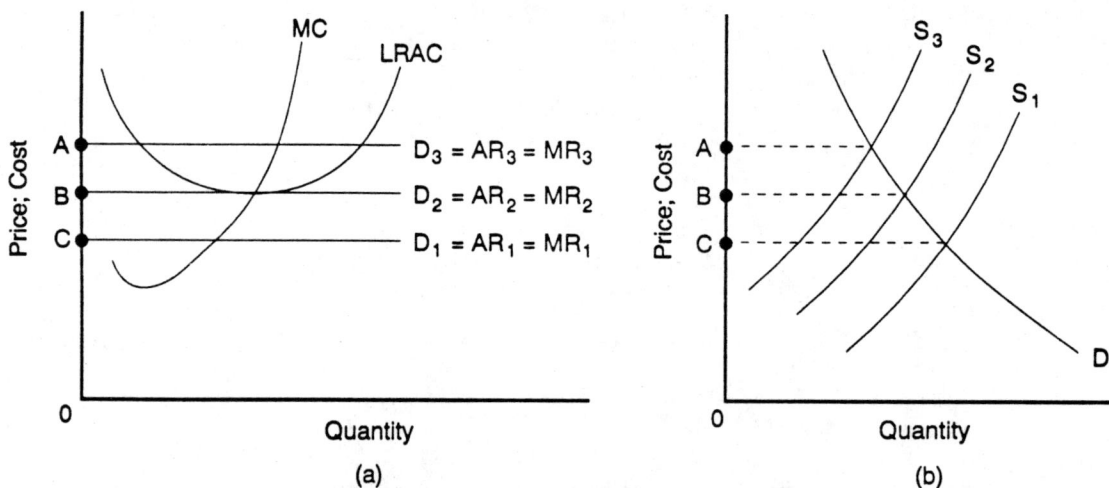

Figure 7-4 Graphs for Problems 10 and 11

11. Review the analysis of long-run equilibrium at normal profits asked for in question 10. But this time use the case of a firm in an increasing-cost industry; then in a decreasing-cost industry. Note carefully how the cost curves and demand curves for the individual firm shift as economic profits vanish and as economic losses vanish.

12. In which situation—an increasing-cost industry, a constant-cost industry, or a decreasing-cost industry—is long-run equilibrium achieved most readily? Why?

13. Give three main reasons why the purely competitive firm is forced to produce at the most technically efficient level of unit cost. What is the difference between productive and allocative efficiency?

14. For a purely competitive economy, what is the significance of price equaling marginal cost?

15. What is consumers' surplus? Producers' surplus? Diagram them using supply and demand determined market equilibrium.

16. What are the three main disadvantages of pure competition?

17. Give reasons why the purely competitive model is relevant and useful to those who are studying the way an economy operates.

PART 4 Self-test

SECTION A True/false questions

T   F   1. The three major characteristics of a purely competitive market situation are (a) no control over price by the individual buyer or seller, (b) homogeneous product, (c) complete freedom of entry of new firms into the industry.

T   F   2. Because of the characteristics of the purely competitive situation, an individual firm in such a market may choose to price its product at or below the prevailing market price, but would never set its price above the prevailing price.

T   F   3. The purely competitive firm's conjectural demand curve slopes downward.

T   F   4. In the short run, the purely competitive firm may obtain economic profits because new firms cannot enter the market and build new plants.

T   F   5. In the third possible situation a purely competitive firm faces in the short run, the firm would incur economic losses; still, it would keep on producing, because its losses would be equal to all of its fixed costs but only part of its variable costs.

T   F   6. The break even point and the shutdown point are the same.

T   F   7. For the purely competitive firm in the short run, the supply curve is its marginal-cost curve throughout its upward-sloping portion.

T   F   8. For a firm in a constant-cost industry in the long run, only a normal profit exists, because new firms entering the industry will eliminate economic profits, increase supply, decrease price, and shift the D = AR = MR curve upward.

T	F	9.	A firm in an increasing-cost industry achieves long-run equilibrium less readily than a firm in a constant-cost industry, because the entry and exit of firms affects not only price but also the cost curves of individual purely competitive firms.
T	F	10.	The purely competitive firm produces at economic capacity because such a firm produces as much as its plant can possibly produce.
T	F	11.	Because in pure competition D, AR and MR are equal and perfectly elastic, when a perfectly competitive firm is earning normal profits in the long run, its marginal cost equals its price.
T	F	12.	Technical efficiency is achieved in the long run under pure competition but not allocative efficiency.
T	F	13.	Long run equilibrium in pure competition maximizes the sum of consumers' and producers' surplus.
T	F	14.	The purely competitive firm may be quick to put known improved technology to use, but because such a firm lacks the large amount of financial capital needed for present-day research and development, it may be less likely than firms in other market situations to develop new technology itself.

SECTION B Multiple-choice questions

1. It is *not* a common characteristic of the purely competitive market situation that
   a. there is complete freedom of entry and exit of firms in the industry.
   b. there are so many firms in the industry that no one firm (or group of firms) has any control over price.
   c. the individual firm definitely finds it to its advantage to advertise its product.
   d. the product the firms produce is homogeneous.

2. A purely competitive firm maximizes its profits (or minimizes its losses) when it produces at the point at which
   a. marginal cost is equal to marginal revenue.
   b. marginal cost intersects the low point on the average-total-cost curve.
   c. the demand, average-revenue, marginal-revenue curve intersects the average-total-cost curve.
   d. profits per unit produced are at a maximum.

3. The break even point is where:
   a. Price is above ATC.
   b. Price is equal to ATC
   c. Price is between ATC and AVC.
   d. Price is equal to AVC.

4. The shut down point is where:
   a. Price is above ATC.
   b. Price is equal to ATC.
   c. Price is between ATC and AVC.
   d. Price is equal to AVC.

5. Which of the following best states why in the short run a firm may decide to continue to produce, even with economic losses?
   a. Price is greater than average variable cost but less than average total cost.
   b. Economic losses are less than fixed costs.
   c. Total revenue is greater than total variable cost but less than total cost.
   d. All of the above are reasons for continuing production.
   e. One of the above is incorrect.

6. Which of the following best describes the relationship between the supply curve and the marginal-cost curve for the purely competitive firm in the short run?
   a. The supply curve is the same as the marginal-cost curve throughout its upward-sloping part.
   b. The supply curve is the same as the marginal-cost curve above the average-variable-cost curve.
   c. The marginal-cost curve and supply curve are the same above the average-total-cost curve.
   d. The marginal-cost curve has nothing to do with the supply curve.

7. In the long run, the purely competitive firm in a constant-cost industry achieves only normal profits, because
   a. new firms entering the industry increase supply, reduce price, and squeeze out the economic profit.
   b. new firms entering the industry do not affect supply since they divide up the existing market, but costs to the firm increase and this squeezes out the economic profit.
   c. economic profits do not exist in the long run, since they cannot exist in the short run because of competition.
   d. in the long run, normal profit is *not* the only situation that can face a purely competitive firm.

8. One of the following is *not* correct. Which?
   a. In a constant-cost industry, the purely competitive firm achieves long-run equilibrium of only normal profits by making only small variations of price.
   b. In an increasing-cost industry, movements of both price and cost achieve normal profits more readily than in a constant-cost industry for the purely competitive firm.
   c. In a decreasing-cost industry, economic profits may exist for longer periods of time because as price falls, so do costs.
   d. All of the above are incorrect.

9. Which of the following explains why in the long run the purely competitive firm produces at lowest possible cost?
   a. There are no economic profits.
   b. The D = AR = MR curve is perfectly elastic and intersects the long-run average-cost curve at its lowest point; thus, the firm produces at full capacity.
   c. There are no advertising costs to add to production costs.
   d. All of the above are correct.

10. Which of the following best explains the significance of the statement that for firms in a purely competitive market, price equals marginal cost?
    a. This has no significance, because profits are maximized or losses minimized when a firm operates at the level at which marginal cost equals *marginal revenue.*
    b. This equation has great significance, because at this point the firm is obtaining economic profits.
    c. This has great significance, because when price equals marginal cost, the allocation of resources is most efficient in producing that combination of goods that consumers prefer.
    d. It is of no significance, because that equality can be obtained only by government manipulation of price.

11. Which best describes the relationship between technical efficiency and allocative efficiency in long run equilibrium under pure competition?
    a. Technical efficiency is greater than allocative.
    b. Allocative efficiency is greater than technical.
    c. They are both maximized.
    d. They have no relationship to each other.

12. Which best describes the relationship between consumers' surplus and producers' surplus in long run equilibrium under pure competition?
    a. The consumers' surplus is greater than the producers' surplus.
    b. The producers' surplus is greater than consumers' surplus.
    c. The sum of consumers' surplus and producers' surplus is maximized (at its greatest).
    d. The difference between consumers' surplus and producers' surplus is at its least.

13. The social disadvantages of a purely competitive market situation do *not* include which one of the following?
    a. The product lacks the variety desired by the public, because of homogeneity in production.
    b. The industry is slow in adopting improved technology that has already been developed.
    c. Like industries in other market situations, purely competitive firms cannot include in their costs and revenues external costs (for example, the cost of pollution control) and benefits.
    d. All of the above are disadvantages of pure competition.

SECTION C Matching questions

I. Match the phrases in column B to the concepts in column A.

Column A
1. Pure competition
2. Homogeneous product
3. Profit maximization
4. Situation of economic profits
5. Situation of normal profits
6. Situation of economic loss *with* production
7. Situation of economic loss with *no* production
8. Short-run supply curve for purely competitive firm
9. Increasing-cost industry
10. Constant-cost industry
11. Decreasing-cost industry
12. Economic capacity

Column B
(a) Marginal-cost curve above average-variable-cost curve
(b) Supply of industry changes without affecting cost curves of individual firm
(c) Price is higher than average total cost
(d) Supply of industry increase; cost curves of individual firm shift up
(e) Price less than average variable cost
(f) Supply of industry increases; cost curves of individual firm shift down
(g) Marginal cost equal to marginal revenue
(h) Price equal to low point on average-total-cost curve
(i) Production at low point of average-total-cost curve
(j) Buyer cannot tell the difference between output of various sellers
(k) Price lower than average total cost but higher than average variable cost
(l) No firm with any control over price

II. Column B lists points, areas, and distances graphed in Figure 7-5. Match the points, areas, and distances in column B to the terms in column A.

Column A
1. Output
2. Price
3. Economic profit
4. Total cost
5. Total revenue
6. Total fixed cost
7. Total variable cost

Column B
(a) 0BEG
(b) 0AFG
(c) C
(d) ABEF
(e) BCDE
(f) G
(g) 0CDF

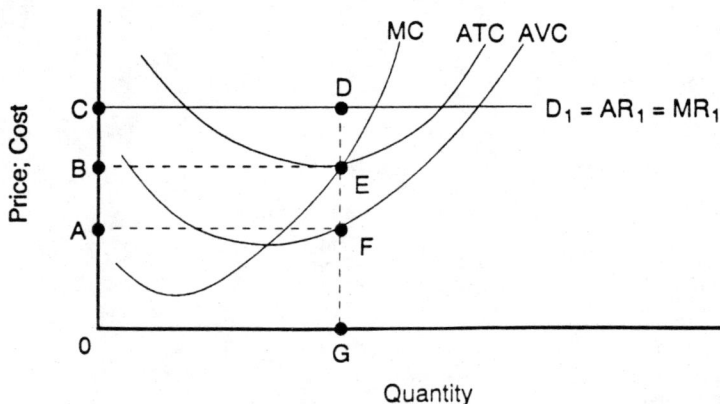

Figure 7-5 Graph for Matching Question 2

ANSWERS

Part 3

8. (a) 1, 1, 1, D, H, UDRS
    (b) 2, 2, 2, C, F, OCQF, OCQF
    (c) 3, 3, 3, B, F, BCLM, VCLN, less than, would
    (c) 4, 4, 4, WXKJ, A, E, AXKI, less than, would not

10. (a) 1, 1, 1, 1, C, up, decrease
    (b) 3, 3, 3, 3, A, down, increase
    (c) 2, 2, 2, 2, B

Part 4

Section A   1, T; 2, F; 3, F; 4, T; 5, F; 6, F; 7, F; 8, F; 9, F; 10, F; 11, T; 12, F; 13, T; 14, T

Section B   1, *c;* 2, *a;* 3, *b;* 4, *d;* 5, *d;* 6, *b;* 7, *a;* 8, *a;* 9, *d;* 10, *c; 11,c; 12, c; 13, b*

Section C   I.   1, l; 2, j; 3, g; 4, c; 5, h; 6, k; 7, e; 8, a; 9, d; 10, b; 11, f; 12, i
             II. 1, f; 2, c; 3, e; 4, a; 5, g; 6, d; 7,b

Application 7   Do We Really Want Competition?
The Farming Mess

PART 1

Reread the section entitled "Summing Up" at the end of Application 7. It offers an excellent review of the application.

Things to Watch For

Agriculture with its large number of firms, homogeneous products, and ease of entry, should come close to being a purely competitive industry. Ever since 1929, however, the U.S. government has actively interfered in this highly competitive market.

Application 7 analyzes supply and demand for agricultural products. The analysis shows why—if this market is allowed to fluctuate on its own—the prices of agricultural products tend to be unstable and farm incomes tend to be variable. The demand for food tends (1) to be very price inelastic, (2) to have low income elasticity, and (3) to be relatively stable. Therefore, variations in supply of food have large effects on food prices. Supply has the dominant role in determining both prices of farm products and farm incomes.

The supply of food is affected by the following factors: (1) The number of farmers is so large that farmers can't get together and work to restrict supply. (2) Farmers' fixed costs constitute a high percentage of their total costs. Therefore, in the short run, it takes very high economic losses to force a farmer to shut down. (3) Changes in weather can readily negate farmers' production plans. (4) Resources of farmers cannot readily be used outside of agriculture. (5) Because of the discontinuity of agricultural production, planning production for the following year is difficult and often attended by risk. (6) Technology, which has mainly been developed outside of agriculture itself, has greatly increased the supply of farm produce. *Note*: Demand and supply for agricultural products are such that they tend to produce great variations of farm income. The tendency is for farm income to be low.

The agricultural support program in effect prior to 1973 was aimed at (1) reducing supply, (2) removing land from production, and (3) stimulating demand so as to keep prices of farm products—and thus farm incomes—high.

Prior to 1973 the government's aim was to support prices of farm products in such a way that they might attain some level of parity with nonfarm prices. But when a government supports the price of a product above the equilibrium price, excess supply of that product is generated. Either demand must be increased or supply decreased.

The application analyzes the various programs undertaken by the Department of Agriculture in an attempt to influence both supply of and demand for farm products. The most important elements in these programs are (1) removing land from production, and

(2) supporting prices. The important points to remember about these farm programs are that (1) they do not help the smaller farmer; and (2) they place a double burden on the consumer in the form of both higher prices and higher taxes.

From 1963 to 1972, as the government paid out large amounts of cash to farmers for withholding land from production, agricultural surpluses declined steadily. Then in 1972 the Soviet Union bought enormous amounts of wheat from the United States and left us without surpluses. This was one of the factors leading to the upsurge in prices of agricultural products in 1973 and 1974. However, although that $1 billion wheat deal with the Soviet Union in 1972 helped fuel this inflation, other factors were involved. As an example of the effects of supply and demand, and also as an assurance that you understand the origins of the present problem of inflationary farm prices, study this agricultural inflation of 1973-1974.

The Agricultural Act of 1973 allowed farmers to plant again land withdrawn from production. It also replaced supported farm prices with direct payments to farmers (paying them the difference between target prices and actual prices). However, the Department of Agriculture reserved the right to reimpose acreage restrictions when it feels they are needed. This law was designed to stimulate agricultural output. But it is hard to foresee how the government will react in the future to any significant fall in agricultural prices and farm incomes.

As bumper crops returned after 1973, farm incomes experienced relative decline. In the Agricultural Acts of 1977, 1983, and 1985, the government returned to active intervention in agricultural markets.

PART 2

Define the following terms and concepts.

1. Low price elasticity of demand
2. Low income elasticity of demand
3. Continuity of production
4. Parity concept
5. Food stamp program
6. Agricultural Act of 1973
7. Agricultural Acts of 1977, 1983, and 1985
8. PIK Program

PART 3

Answer the following questions and problems.

1. How does the market for agricultural products fit the basic characteristics of the purely competitive market?

2. What major characteristics of the demand for farm products help account for fluctuating and unstable prices and low farm incomes?

3. Using Figure A7-1, draw curves and explain why with low price elasticity and low income elasticity, variations in supply of farm products have large effects on the price of these products.

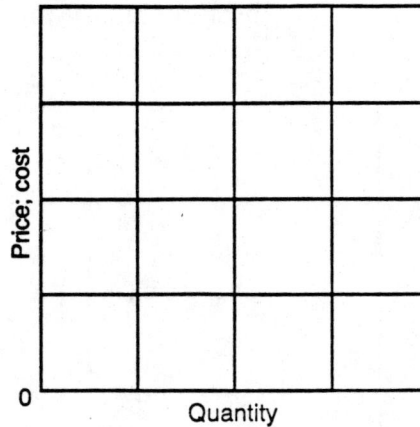

Figure A7-1 Graph for Problem 3

4. List the various factors that influence agricultural supply, both in the short run and in the long run, and explain why they influence it. In your analysis, emphasize the point that supply tends to be outside the control of the farmer and tends to increase.

5. Why has technological change had an uneven impact on different groups of farmers?

6. Using your analysis from problems 2 and 3, on demand, and from problem 4, on supply, explain why agricultural prices tend to be highly variable and farm incomes to be low.

7. Using Figure A7-2, explain what happens when the government supports prices of a given farm product.

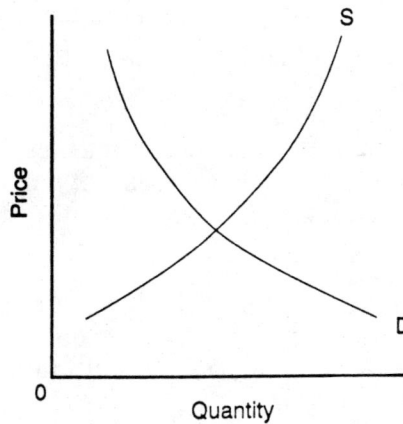

Figure A7-2 Graph for Problem 8

8. The government's program of supporting prices of farm products is of little help to the small farmer and places a double burden on the consumer. Explain why.

9. Using Figure A7-3, demonstrate the inflationary impact of the 1972 Soviet wheat deal.

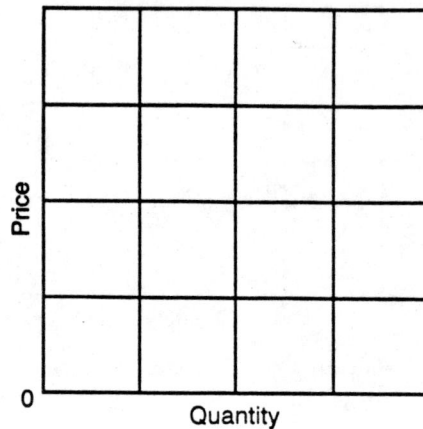

Figure A7-3 Graph for Problem 13

PART 4 Self-test

SECTION A True/false questions

T   F   1. A prime reason why the government interfered in the market for farm products is that despite the purely competitive market situation, farmers could not provide enough food for the Canadian population because the prices they got for their produce were so low.

T   F   2. On the demand side of the market for farm products, both price elasticity and income elasticity of demand are very low. This means that demand tends to be the stable factor in pricing of farm products.

T   F   3. On the supply side of the market for farm products, both price elasticity and income elasticity of demand are very low. This means that demand tends to be the stable factor in pricing of farm products.

T   F   4. In both the short and the long run, resources of farmers are very mobile, in that farmers can easily shift their resources to the production of other, nonagricultural products.

T   F   5. Discontinuity of agricultural production means that farmers have effective control over output because they can stop production at any point.

T   F   6. Prior to 1973 the government's farm program aimed at raising prices of farm products above equilibrium. This resulted in excess demand and the need to reduce demand and increase supply.

T   F   7. After the 1973 Agricultural Act, the government learned from past experiences and stopped interfering in agricultural markets.

T   F   8. Even under a conserative republican administration in the 1980's, the agricultural aid program seemed to continue to spend much and achieve little.

SECTION B Multiple-choice questions

1. During which one of the following periods did farmers in the North America experience conditions for agriculture which were different from conditions in the other periods?
   a. 1900-1920
   b. 1920-1940
   c. 1940-1950
   d. 1950-1970

2. Which of the following statements does *not* characterize the market structure of Canadian agriculture?
   a. The market is purely competitive, with large numbers of firms, a homogeneous product, and complete freedom of entry.
   b. Demand for agricultural products is price inelastic; that is, quantity demanded increases only slightly as price declines.
   c. In the long run, farmers' resources are highly mobile, in that farmers can remove their resources from agriculture as losses become evident.
   d. There are few good substitutes for agricultural products.

3. Which of the following statements does *not* explain why demand for agricultural products tends to be stable?
   a. Demand for agricultural products tends to be price inelastic, because farm products are a necessity and there are few good substitutes.
   b. Demand for agricultural products tends to be income inelastic, so that demand for farm products responds only slightly to economic growth.
   c. With people's worry about obesity increasing, it is unlikely that they will prefer greater amounts of food in the future.
   d. Agriculture is characterized by discontinuity in production.

4. The supply of agricultural products tends to be outside the control of farmers for all but which one of the following reasons?
   a. Agricultural products are an example of continuous production.
   b. Weather is variable and uncontrollable.
   c. The number of farmers is too great to permit them to get together and deliberately restrict supply.
   d. Agricultural resources are highly immobile into and out of agriculture.

5. Which of the following statements about the government's agricultural support program prior to 1973 is *not* true?
   a. Government price supports for farm products placed a double burden on the consumer, in the form of both higher prices and higher taxes.
   b. The program was successful in raising the income of the small farmer.
   c. Farmers were able to offset to some extent the decreases in supply that resulted from removing acreage from production by keeping in production the most fertile land and by increasing the use of fertilizer.
   d. Marginal utility divided by income is irrelevant.

6. The Canadian government's program of support for prices of farm products tended to benefit the larger farmer but not the smaller farmer because of which one of the following?
   a. The laws exempted farms smaller than a certain size.
   b. The prices paid to the larger farmers for price support for their products were larger than those paid to the smaller farmers for theirs.
   c. Small farmers did not have enough resources (land and capital or skills) to begin with. That meant that their incomes were small even with aid from the government's programs.
   d. The Department of Agriculture was trying to get these small, inefficiently run farms out of agriculture. Therefore, they deliberately stacked the cards against the small farmer.

7. Which one of the following is not part of government policy toward agriculture after 1973?
   a. Efforts to stimulate demand for agricultural products.
   b. Efforts to reduce agricultural supply.
   c. Efforts to remove government from the agricultural industry.
   d. Efforts to cause direct income support for farmers.

SECTION C Matching questions

Match the phrases in column B to the terms in column A.

Column A	Column B
1. Low price elasticity	(a) When price changes, quantity demanded changes by small amounts
2. Low income elasticity	(b) In manufacturing, production, is a continuous process; in agriculture, time elapses between planting and harvesting
3. Parity	
4. Continuity of production	(c) When income increases, demand increases by small amounts
5. Food stamp program	(d) Established a set of target prices and direct payments to farmers instead of maintaining supported prices
6. Agricultural Act of 1973	(e) Enables low-income people to obtain stamps from the government and exchange them for food at stores
	(f) Prices of what farmers sell keep pace with prices of what farmers buy

ANSWERS

Part 4

Section A   1, F; 2, T; 3, T; 4, F; 5, F; 6, F; 7, F; 8, T
Section B   1, b; 2, c; 3, d; 4, a; 5, b; 6, c; 7, c
Section C   1, a; 2, c;3,f;4,b;5,e;6,d

CHAPTER 8   *Pure Monopoly: The Other Extreme*

Application 8   *Regulation Versus Deregulation: When are Airline Markets Contestable?*

PART 1

Reread the sections entitled "Summing Up" at the end of Chapter 8 as well as Application 8. They offer an excellent review of the chapter and application.

Things to Watch For

Chapter 8

Chapter 8 first defines **pure monopoly**: a situation in which there's only one firm in the industry and the firm produces a product for which there are no good substitutes. Then it discusses the various restraints on the monopoly firm as to price and profit manipulation. Note: Although the firm has complete control over supply, when it comes to setting price and achieving profits, it is restrained by demand, costs, and substitutability of product.

The fact that only one firm exists in a monopolistic industry must mean that other firms are completely barred from entering. The text describes six of the main kinds of barriers to entry.

Having described monopoly conditions, the chapter analyzes the shape of the demand curve and marginal-revenue curve of the monopolistic firm. Since the monopoly's demand curve is the industry's demand curve, the curve slopes down to the right. Therefore, to sell more, the monopoly must lower price. Because of this, its marginal-revenue curve is separate from and declines more rapidly than its demand curve.

The chapter shows how to add cost curves to revenue curves and analyzes the situation of the purely monopolistic firm in the short run. The monopoly firm encounters the same four possible cost-profit combinations as the purely competitive firm. But in the case of the monopoly, the demand curve lies above the marginal-revenue curve. Like the purely competitive firm, the monopoly, maximizes profits or minimizes losses at the level of output at which marginal cost equals marginal revenue. However, the monopoly is a price seeker and its price on the demand curve is greater than marginal cost.

In the long run the monopoly firm encounters two possible situations. The most probable is *economic profit*. (Since there are significant barriers to entry into the industry, new firms cannot enter to draw away economic profits through competition.) The monopoly firm may also earn a *normal profit*. The exit of an unprofitable firm from the industry rules out the possibility of economic losses.

The chapter compares the economic performances of purely competitive industries and purely monopolistic ones. If we assume that the pure monopolist has the same set of costs as those of the purely competitive industry, the equilibrium monopoly price is higher, output lower and average costs are higher. Using the concepts of producers' and consumers' surplus under monopoly, the producers' surplus increases with higher monopoly prices but the consumers' surplus decreases. In addition, there is a dead weight loss to society, one not captured by either producers or consumers. Sometimes, when we compare the two market situations, we do not assume that cost curves are the same for both, because the nature of technology may require that a firm be large before it can take advantage of economies of scale. If average costs thus fall as plants grow larger, there is a case of *natural monopoly*. It is technological efficiency and economies of scale that seem to offer the primary advantage of large size. But the mere fact of largeness does not necessarily imply monopoly, nor can a firm increase its efficiency by adding to its size beyond the point at which it attains economies of scale. Given the restraints of technological efficiency, more competition is still preferable to less.

Note that if it's true that in pure monopoly the demand curve slopes down to the right (because, to keep on selling more, a monopoly firm must lower its price), and that the marginal-revenue curve therefore lies below the demand curve, and that price always lies above the marginal-revenue curve, then it must also be true that in the long run, the monopoly firm's price cannot equal its marginal cost, as is the case for the purely competitive firm. This means that in a purely monopolistic industry there is an inefficient allocation of resources. The reason is that the monopoly firm produces less than the consumer wants: Marginal cost, measuring what is given up, is less than price, which is the value consumers put on the last unit the firm produces.

The subject of the **regulated monopoly** is important because almost all of today's pure monopolies are regulated; public utilities are regulated monopolies, for example. Prices of products of the public utility companies are set by regulatory commissions, which theoretically, price the products in such a way as to prevent the firms from exploiting their monopolistic positions. The commission sets prices at the point at which average revenue equals average cost, and the firms reap only a normal profit. As a result, prices of the utilities are lower and output is greater than they would be if there were no regulation. (Theoretically, that is.)

The chapter ends with a discussion of **price discrimination,** or charging different prices to different customers for the same product. Not every seller can price-discriminate between customers. Special conditions are needed. (1) Monopoly power must exist, so that individual firms have the ability to influence price. (2) The product must be of such a nature that the customer who is charged the lower price cannot resell the product. (3) The elasticity of one customer's demand for the product must be different from the elasticity of other customers' demand for it. Otherwise, the seller who practiced the price discrimination would not be able to increase profits.

When a monopoly firm is able to price-discriminate, it maximizes its profits when it charges in each market a price that is such that marginal cost equals marginal revenue. In a given market, the lower the price elasticity of demand, the higher the price the firm will charge.

Finally, though the dead weight loss is not affected, the producers' surplus increases at the expense of consumers' surplus with price discrimination by monopoly firms.

Application 8

Application 8 examines some of the controversies over regulation or deregulation within the airline industry. A key concept in understanding the effects of either regulation or deregulation is **contestable markets** or the ability of firms to readily enter and leave markets in response to profits or losses. If deregulation does not improve contestability of markets then the gains to be made from moving from a monopoly situation are unlikely to occur. The application explores what happened with airline deregulation and troubles that may be occuring in the deregulation of the industry, especially its increased concentration and the difficulty for new firms in entering due to lack of airport facilities.

PART 2

Define the following terms and concepts.

1. Pure monopoly
2. Natural monopoly
3. Regulated monopoly
4. Barriers to entry
5. Allocative inefficiency
6. Monopoly power
7. Price discrimination
8. Perfect price discrimination
9. Third degree price discrimination
10. Contestable market
11. Perfectly contestable market

PART 3

Answer the following questions and problems.

1. Define pure monopoly and discuss the various factors that prevent the monopolistic firm from being able to manipulate price and profits as much as it might wish.

2. List six barriers to entry and explain how they work. Pick four industries and discuss barriers to entry that might exist in them.

3. In a situation of pure monopoly, why aren't the demand and marginal-revenue curves the same?

4. In the four-part diagram of Figure 8-1, draw demand, marginal revenue, and cost curves showing the four possible profit or loss situations that the purely monopolistic firm might encounter in the short run. Explain each of these possible situations.

5. Figure 8-2 shows the cost and revenue curves for the purely monopolistic firm in the long run. Price is _____ and output is _____. Total revenue is _____. Total cost is _____. The monopolist obtains a(n) (*economic profit/normal profit/ economic loss*) equal to _____. (The answers are given after Part 4.)

6. Figure 8-3 shows one set of cost curves and two demand-average-revenue curves: one for the purely monopolistic firm and one for the purely competitive firm. Which is the demand curve for the monopoly, D_1 or D_2, and which is the demand curve for the competitive firm, D_1 or D_2? Price for the monopoly firm is _____; for the competitive firm _____. Output for the monopoly is _____; for the competitive firm _____. Cost per unit for the monopoly is _____; for the competitive firm _____. (The answers are given after Part 4.)

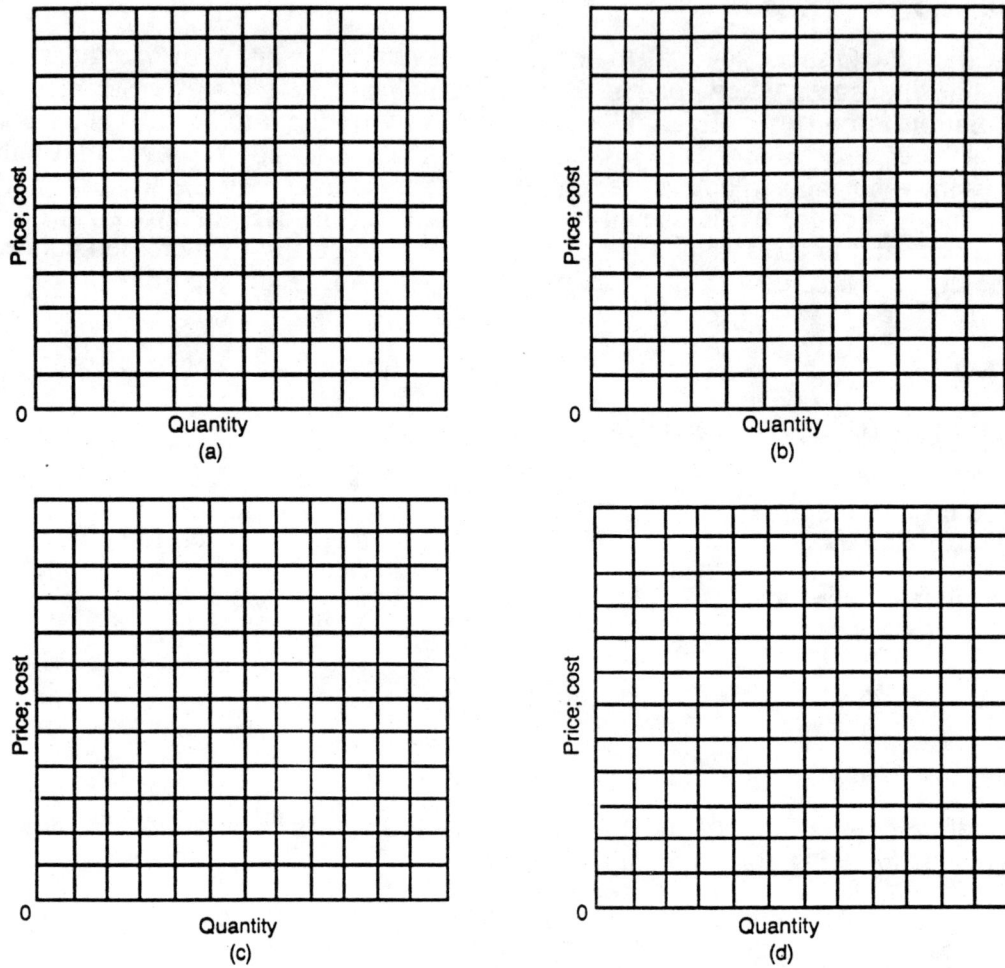

Figure 8-1 Graphs for Problem 4

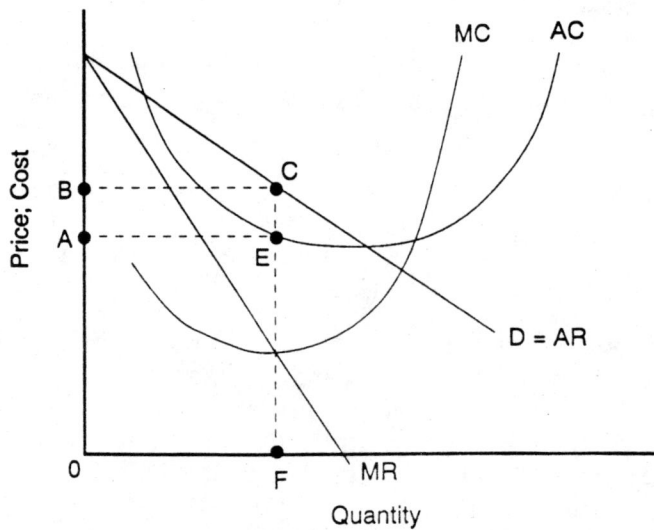

Figure 8-2 Graph for Problem 5

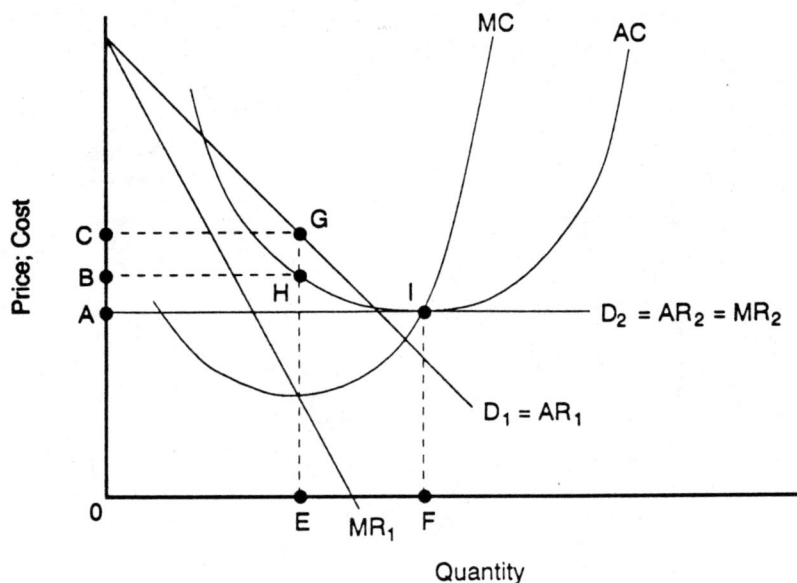

Figure 8-3 Graph for Problems 6 and 7

7. Use TR/TC graphs to show the four possible short-run equilibria for pure monopoly. Compare your equilibrias with those shown in question 4 above.

8. Using diagrams show how the consumer surplus and producer surplus change under pure monopoly. What area would represent the dead weight loss to society?

9. Which of the two market structure—purely competitive or purely monopolistic—would have the greater advantage with respect to the industry's likelihood of
   a. adopting improved technology? Why?
   b. developing new technology? Why?

10. Figure 8-4 compares regulated and unregulated monopolies. In the presence of regulation, price of the monopoly's product would be _____ and quantity produced _____. In the absence of regulation, price would be _____ and quantity produced _____. With regulation, the monopoly's price would be (*higher/lower*) and output (*higher/lower*) than without it. (The answers are given after Part 4.) Why is this difficult to achieve in practice?

11. What conditions must hold in order for price discrimination to be possible?

12. In Figure 8-5 draw the relevant demand, revenue, and marginal-cost curves to show how price discrimination can maximize profits for a monopolistic firm. If you have any difficulties with drawing the curves, refer to Figure 8-11 in the text.

13. Give three examples of price discrimination. Using the theory presented in the text, explain how price discrimination works.

14. Define contestable markets and show how this concept applies to deregulation.

15. What advantages should one expect from deregulation in the airline industry? What factor seems to limit contestability in a deregulated airline industry?

16. Explain why the price charged by a monopoly is likely to be *lower* than pure competition. Illustrate with an appropriate graph.

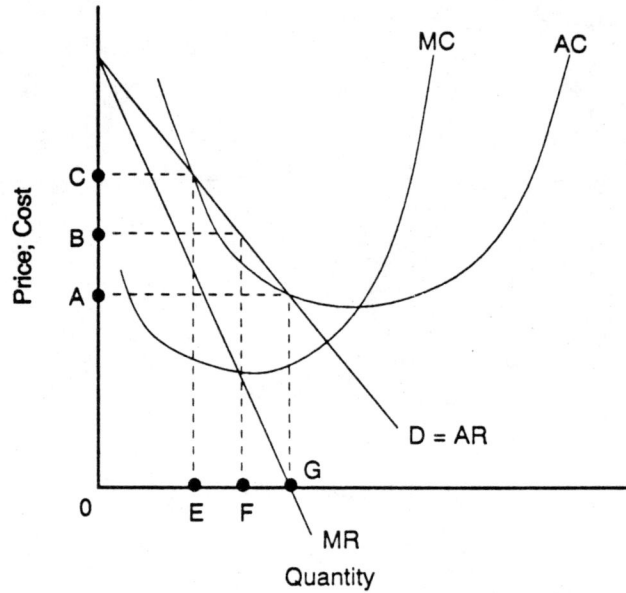

Figure 8-4 Graph for Problem 9

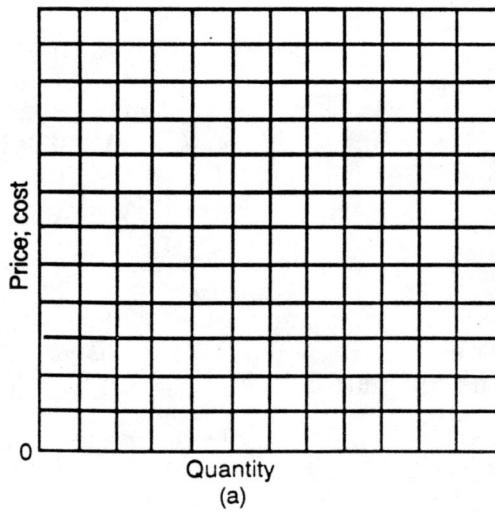

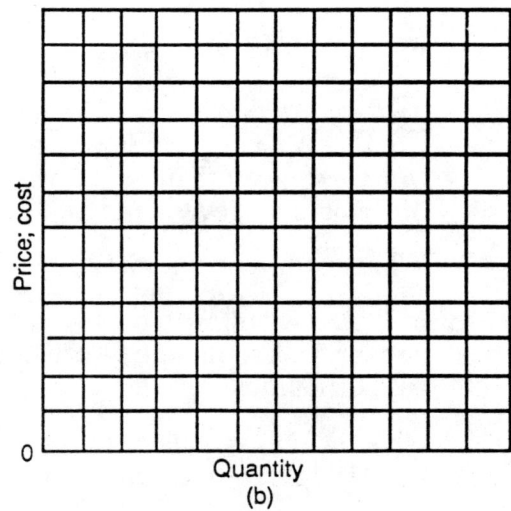

Figure 8-5 Graphs for Problem 11

PART 4 Self-test

SECTION A True/false questions

T F 1. Because there is only one firm in a pure monopoly, that single monopolistic firm can dictate both the price of the product and the quantity demanded.

T F 2. For firms in a purely competitive market, demand, average revenue, and marginal revenue are the same and are perfectly elastic, because the individual firm has no control over price. However, in a pure monopoly, because the firm does have control over price, the demand-average-revenue curve slopes down to the right, and the marginal-revenue curve lies below it.

T F 3. Because there is only one firm in a pure monopoly, in the short run that firm can incur no economic losses.

T F 4. Because the purely monopolistic firm maximizes profits by producing the rate of output at which marginal cost is equal to marginal revenue, it also produces what consumers want and does so with the most efficient allocation of resources.

T F 5. Given the same cost curves, the purely competitive firm sells its output at a lower price than the purely monopolistic firm, but the monopoly produces more output.

T F 6. In the long run the purely competitive firm obtains only a normal profit whereas the purely monopolistic firm is likely to obtain an economic profit.

T F 7. In pure monopoly consumers' surplus declines and producers' surplus declines because of dead weight losses.

T F 8. Some people say that the fact that the development of new advances in technology today requires huge sums of money is an argument in favor of largeness. The larger the firm, they say, the greater the amount of money available and therefore the more rapid the development of new technology. This argument *cannot* be refuted.

T F 9. To enable a monopolistic firm (such as a utility company) to earn normal profits, a regulatory commission must set the price of the firm's product at the point at which marginal cost equals average cost.

T F 10. In order for a firm to be able to price-discriminate, the following conditions must exist, the firm must have monopoly power, the consumer who bought at the lower price must be unable to resell to the consumer who bought at a higher price, and there must be differing price elasticities of demand.

T F 11. A price-discriminating firm charges a higher price to the customer that has the higher price elasticity of demand.

Chapter 8/Application 8   73

T	F	12.	As a purely monopolistic firm price discriminates, consumers' surplus declines while producers' surplus increases.
T	F	13.	The effort made by some regulatory commissions to maintain the status quo in a given public utility has hurt both the consumer and the industry itself.
T	F	14.	A principle barrier to entry in the airline industry is limitation of landing spaces in airports.
T	F	15.	After deregulation, all fears of monopolizaton disappeared as the number of airlines increased and decentralization occurred.

SECTION B Multiple-choice questions

1. Although the purely monopolistic firm is the only firm in the industry, there are restraints on a monopoly's ability to change price and profits. Which one of the following is *not* such a restraint?
   a. A monopolistic firm is constrained by demand for the product
   b. A monopolistic firm has competition from other industries that produce close substitutes.
   c. The federal government restricts pure monopolies to making only a normal profit.
   d. A monopolistic firm is constrained by the costs of production

2. Which of the following is a barrier to entry of new firms into an industry?
   a. A monopolistic firm has control over patents and secret processes.
   b. A monopolistic firm uses price discrimination in economic warfare.
   c. A monopolistic firm controls sources of supply.
   d. New firms have to pay higher advertising costs per unit produced than established firms do.
   e. All of the above are obstacles to entry.

3. For the purely monopolistic firm during the short run, which of the following is *not* true?
   a. The firm maximizes profits and minimizes losses by producing at that point at which marginal costs are equal to marginal revenue.
   b. Price is higher than marginal cost.
   c. The firm is faced by the same four possible profit or loss situations that confront the purely competitive firm in the short run.
   d. The firm sets its price at the point at which average revenue equals average total cost in all situations.

4. For the purely monopolistic firm in the long run, which of the following is *not* true.
   a. The firm is likely to obtain an economic profit.
   b. The firm usually produces at less than full capacity–that is, at some scale that is less than the most efficient one.
   c. The firm's marginal-revenue curve is below its demand-average-revenue curve.
   d. The firm incurs economic losses, because if the firm left the industry, the industry itself would disappear.

5. Comparing pure competition and pure monopoly in the long run and assuming the same cost curves, which of the following is true?
   a. Since the purely monopolistic firm's price is higher than its marginal cost, resources are allocated inefficiently from the social point of view, so that consumers get less than they prefer. This is not true of the purely competitive firm.
   b. The purely monopolistic firm's price is lower and its output higher than the purely competitive firm's.
   c. The purely monopolistic firm's costs are lower than the purely competitive firm's.
   d. The competitive industry's price in the long run is higher than that of the purely monopolistic industry.

6. If you were comparing pure monopoly and pure competition in their ability to foster the development and adoption of new technologies, which one of the following points should you *not* try to make?
   a. If one were to divide a purely monopolistic firm into enough firms to duplicate a situation of pure competition, one would perhaps have to sacrifice economies of scale and/or the use of new technology.
   b. Purely monopolistic firms adopt improved technology more quickly than purely competitive firms do, and in the process they abandon obsolete plant and equipment.
   c. At times, smaller firms pioneer during the high-risk, low-cost stage of development of an innovation. They then turn the new project over to a large firm, which takes it through the low-risk but high-cost perfecting stage.
   d. Larger firms may expect higher rates of return and invest more heavily in innovative activities.

7. When a monopolistic firm is under the control of a regulatory commission,
   a. price is at the same level as it would be under pure competition.
   b. price is at the same level as it would be in an unregulated pure monopoly, but the government taxes away the economic profit of the regulated monopoly.
   c. price is theoretically set at the level at which average revenue equals average cost, and only a normal profit exists.
   d. price may be higher than it would be in an unregulated monopoly, but output is greater.

8. A pure monopoly is made a government-franchised monopoly and is regulated because
   a. having more than one firm in the industry would be inefficient and inconvenient to customers, but not regulating the industry might produce economic profits.
   b. the law says that the federal government must regulate all pure monopolies, regardless of what they produce.
   c. the communists in our government are trying to subvert the American way of life.
   d. private unregulated monopolies are unable to establish their prices

9. Which one of the following statements describes price discrimination most accurately?
   a. All business firms, regardless of their market situation, can engage in price discrimination.
   b. Any business firm with monopoly power can price-discriminate between any of its customers.
   c. Any business firm with monopoly power can price-discriminate between any of its customers so long as the customer who pays the lower price cannot resell the commodity to a customer who pays a higher price.
   d. Any business firm with monopoly power can price-discriminate between any of its customers so long as the customer who pays the lower price cannot resell the commodity to a customer who pays a higher price and so long as elasticity of demand is not the same for both customers.

10. Suppose that a certain firm is selling in two markets and is price discriminating between them. Price will be
    a. higher in the market in which price elasticity of demand is higher.
    b. higher in the market in which price elasticity of demand is lower.
    c. higher in the market in which there is a greater number of close substitutes.
    d. none of the above, because price discrimination has nothing to do with either price elasticity of demand or product substitutability.

11. Which one of the following factors has decreased contestability in the airline industry?
    a. Re-establishment of government regulation.
    b. Slow rate of building of new and expansion of existing airports.
    c. Increase in the number of airlines.
    d. Increase in the number of passangers.

12. Which one of the following was achieved through deregulation of the airline industry?
    a. An increase in consumers' and producers' surplus.
    b. An increase in airline safety.
    c. A sharp increase in airport space.
    d. A reduction in mergers and concentration.

13. Under pure monopoly
    a. Producers' surplus increases by a greater amount than consumers' surplus decreases.
    b. Producers' surplus increases by a smaller amount than consumers' surplus decreases.
    c. Producers' surplus increases by the same amount as consumers' surplus decreases.
    d. Consumers' surplus increases.

14. Whan a pure monopolist price discriminates
    a. Producers' surplus increases by a greater amount than consumers' surplus decreases.
    b. Producers' surplus increases by a smaller amount than consumers' surplus decreases.
    c. Producers' surplus increases by the same amount as consumers' surplus decreases.
    d. Consumers' surplus increases.

SECTION C Matching questions

I. Match the phrases in column B to the terms in column A.

Column A
1. Pure monopoly
2. Regulated monopoly
3. Price discrimination
4. Profit maximization
5. Price under pure monopoly

Column B
(a) Prices paid vary by customer; these differences are not justified by differences in cost
(b) A situation in which there is only one firm in the industry
(c) Lies above marginal cost
(d) The firm produces the amount of output that makes it possible for its marginal cost to equal its marginal revenue
(e) To prevent the monopolistic firm from exploiting the public, the government sets the price the firm can charge

II. Column B lists points, areas, and distances graphed in Figure 8-3. Match the points, areas, and distances in column B to the terms in column A.

Column A
1. Price under monopoly
2. Price under competition
3. Output under monopoly
4. Output under competition
5. Total revenue under monopoly
6. Economic profit under monopoly

Column B
(a) F
(b) BCGH
(c) A
(d) C
(e) 0CGE
(f) E

ANSWERS

Part 3

5. B, F, 0BCF, 0AEF, economic profit, ABCE
6. D_1, D_2, C, A, E, F, B, A
10. A, G, B, F, lower, higher

Part 4

Section A 1, F; 2, T; 3, F; 4, F; 5, F; 6, T; 7, T; 8, F; 9, F; 10, T; 11, F; 12, T; 13, T; 14, T; 15, F
Section B 1, c; 2, e; 3, d; 4, d; 5, a; 6, b; 7, c; 8, a; 9, d; 10, b; 11, b; 12, a; 13, b; 14, c
Section C I. 1, b; 2, e; 3, a; 4, d; 5, c;
          II. 1, d; 2, c; 3, f; 4, a; 5, e; 6, b

CHAPTER 9   *Imperfect Competition: Monopolistic Competition and Product Differentiation*

PART 1

Reread the section entitled "Summing Up" at the end of Chapter 9. It provides an excellent review of the chapter.

Things to Watch For

Chapter 9

The main difference between **monopolistic competition** and pure competition is in the area of *product differentiation*. The most important form of differentiation of products is location—though there *are* other kinds of differentiation. Monopolistically competitive business firms use advertising to stress the feature that makes one product differ from others; but their advertising is primarily local in appeal. An industry that is monopolistically competitive is also characterized by (1) many small firms, and (2) ease of entry into and exit from the field. These factors limit an individual firm's ability to exploit product differentiation.

Chapter 9 analyzes the curves showing demand (D), average revenue (AR), and marginal revenue (MR) for a monopolistically competitive firm. Because such a firm can differentiate its product and thus has some control over price, demand and average revenue are not perfectly elastic. The MR curve slopes more steeply and lies below the demand-average-revenue (D = AR) curve. Because new firms can enter the industry easily and because at any time many firms already have a share of it, these curves for monopolistic competitors are more elastic than they are for pure monopolists. In the short run, the monopolistically competitive firm encounters the same four profit or loss situations as firms in other market classifications. The firm may earn (1) an economic profit, (2) a normal profit, (3) just enough to cover variable costs plus some fixed costs (resulting in an economic loss), or (4) not enough to cover even variable costs (resulting in shutdown).

In the long run, it's probable that the typical monopolistic competitor will make only a normal profit. The ease with which firms can enter brings firms into a monopolistically competitive market to get a share of the economic profits. As the market comes to be shared by a larger and larger number of firms, the demand for the output of the typical firm is lowered. The economic profit is eliminated, and only a normal profit remains. Losses can be eliminated only by the exit of firms. However, it is possible for an atypical firm to differentiate its product so effectively that it can keep on making economic profits even in the long run.

When one compares monopolistic competition with pure competition, one sees that many of the criticisms of pure monopoly also apply here. Compare a purely competitive firm with a monopolistically competitive one; assume the same cost curves for both firms. (Since both firms are small, assuming similar cost curves for them seems to be a realistic idea.) The purely competitive firm receives a lower price for its product, produces a larger output, and does it at a lower cost than the monopolistically competitive firm. Since in monopolistic competition price is above marginal cost, there is also an inefficient allocation of resources; companies do not use their resources to produce that combination of goods and services that consumers prefer. However, since both purely competitive and monopolistically competitive firms are highly competitive, the differences between them may not be large enough to be significant.

The most serious criticism of monopolistic competition is that of the "wastes of monopolistic competition." These firms produce at higher (than pure competition) cost at less than economic capacity. Some unused capacity is common. The amount of excess capacity depends on the elasticity of demand. For most monopolistically competitive industries, these elasticities are high and the wastes from excess capacity are probably low. The conclusion of the chapter is that this ability to minimize competition by differentiating products is limited. Thus, for industries that have differentiated products, monopolistic competition is as close as one can get to competition.

PART 2

Define the following terms and concepts.

1. Monopolistic competition
2. Product differentiation
3. Waste of monopolistic competition and the excess capacity theorem

PART 3

Answer the following questions and problems.

1. Describe the characteristics of monopolistic competition. Using two industries as examples, illustrate these characteristics.

2. In what ways can the monopolistically competitive firm accentuate the features that make its product different from other firms' products? Why would the firm wish to do so? What factors limit the firm in its ability to do so?

3. Use Figure 9-1 to draw curves showing demand, average revenue, and marginal revenue for business firms in the three market classifications studied so far. Explain why the curves for monopolistically competitive firms slope the way they do.

4. In part (a) of Figure 9-2, draw the cost and revenue curves showing a monopolistically competitive firm making a normal profit. In part (b) illustrate the possibility of its making an economic profit. Explain why these two possibilities exist.

5. Compare monopolistic competition with pure competition in terms of economic performance. Is it realistic to assume that firms in both classifications have the same cost curves? Why? Are these differences in economic performance significant? Why?

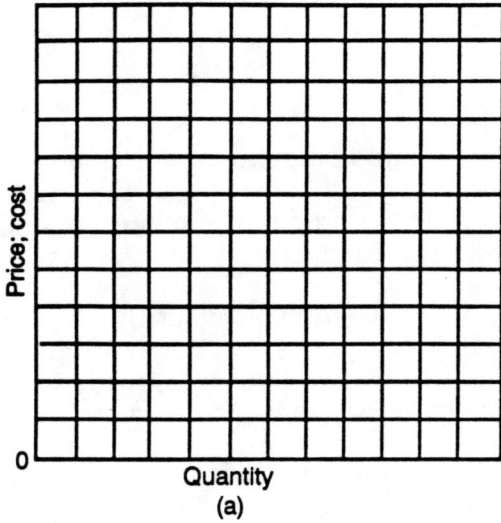

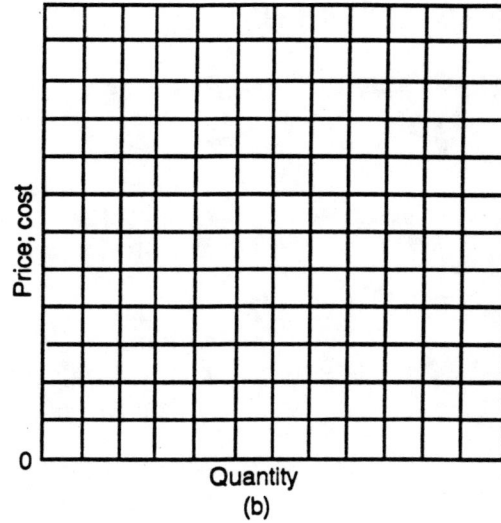

Figure 9-1 Graphs for Problem 3

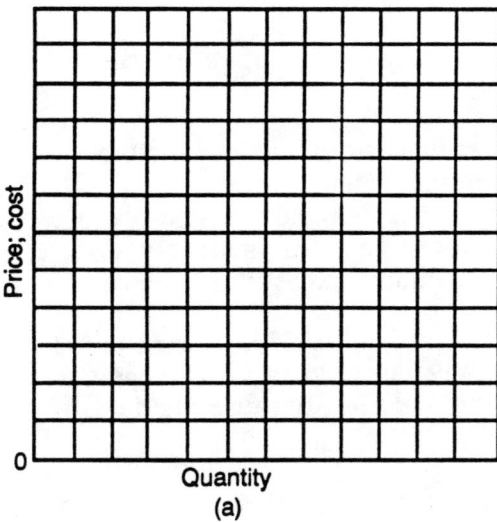

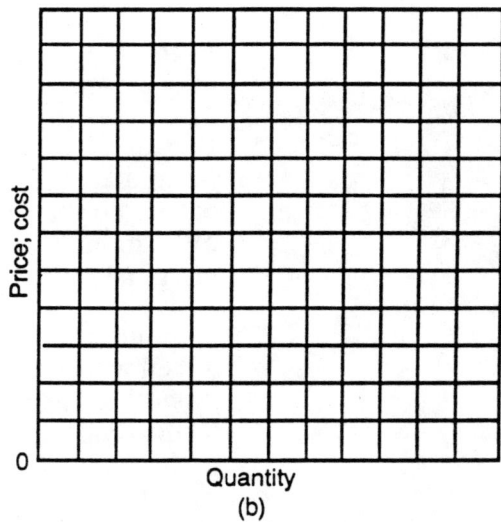

Figure 9-2 Graphs for Problem 4

6. What are the most important forms of differentiation used in monopolistic competition? Discuss the way these forms of differentiation limit the individual firm's control over prices.

7. What determines the "wastes of monopolistic competition?" According to Leonard Weiss, are these wastes likely to be very large?

8. If there are too many firms in monopolistic competition competing against each other, why isn't the price *lower* than pure competition? Illustrate with an appropriate graph.

PART 4 Self-test

SECTION A True/false questions

T   F   1. The main difference between pure competition and monopolistic competition is that whereas monopolistically competitive firms can differentiate their products from the products of other firms in the industry, purely competitive firms cannot.

T   F   2. The ability of a monopolistically competitive firm to exploit product differentiation and charge prices that differ from prices charged by other firms is limited by two things: (a) many firms in the industry, and (b) the ease of entry into the industry.

T   F   3. Monopolistically competitive firms maximize their profits by producing output up to the point at which profit per unit is largest.

T   F   4. Because of ease of entry into the industry and the large number of firms in the industry, a monopolistically competitive firm cannot make an economic profit in the short run.

T   F   5. In the long run, the monopolistically competitive firm can make only a normal profit.

T   F   6. Because the advantage to be had from product differentiation is limited by the fact that there are many firms in the industry and entry into the industry is easy, the demand-average-revenue curve of a monopolistically competitive firm is highly elastic, and marginal revenue is equal to demand and average revenue.

T   F   7. Although a monopolistically competitive firm's profits are maximized when its marginal cost equals its marginal revenue, the price it charges is greater than marginal cost, because the demand curve for its product is not perfectly elastic.

T   F   8. The monopolistically competitive firm charges higher prices and produces less output than the purely competitive firm.

T   F   9. One problem with monopolistic competition is the so-called waste that results from the monopolistically competitive firm's operating at less than full capacity in the long run.

T   F   10. It is not very realistic to assume that a monopolistically competitive firm has the same cost curves as a purely competitive one.

T   F   11. In an industry that is monopolistically competitive, three kinds of product differentiation are location, differences in quality, and brand names.

T   F   12. Advertising is an important method of stressing product differentiation.

T   F   13. Differences in location cause consumers to pay scant regard to variations in price between one firm and another.

T   F   14. The wastes of monopolistic competition stem directly from the use of advertising.

SECTION B Multiple-choice questions

1. Which of the following is *not* a characteristic of monopolistic competition?
   a. Many firms
   b. Differentiated product
   c. Relative ease of entry
   d. National advertising

2. In the short run in monopolistic competition, profits are maximized or losses minimized when
   a. price equals demand.
   b. marginal cost equals marginal revenue.
   c. profit per unit is at its highest.
   d. marginal cost equals average total cost.

3. Which of the following is *not* a form of product differentiation?
   a. Location
   b. Differences in quality
   c. Government-granted monopoly franchise
   d. Differences in services
   e. Brand or store names

4. In monopolistic competition, the elasticity of demand for the firm's product is
   a. less than in pure competition, but greater than in pure monopoly.
   b. greater than in pure competition, but less than in pure monopoly.
   c. greater than it is in both pure competition and pure monopoly.
   d. less than it is in both pure competition and pure monopoly.

5. For firms in an industry that is monopolistically competitive, which one of the following is true of prices?
   a. Prices are greater than marginal cost.
   b. Prices are equal to marginal cost.
   c. Prices are less than marginal cost.
   d. Price has no special relationship to marginal cost.

6. In the long run, a monopolistically competitive firm will encounter two possible profit or loss situations. These are
   a. the probability of economic profits and the possibility of only normal profits.
   b. the probability of normal profits and the possibility of economic profits.
   c. the probability of normal profits and the possibility of economic losses.
   d. the probability of economic losses and the possibility of normal profits.

7. In monopolistic competition, the relationship between price and marginal cost shows which one of the following to be true?
   a. Resources are not allocated efficiently enough for the industry to produce that combination of goods and services that consumers prefer.
   b. Resources are allocated efficiently, so that the industry produces that combination of goods and services that consumers prefer.
   c. The relationship of price and marginal cost in monopolistic competition holds no special significance with respect to efficiency in the allocation of resources.
   d. The relationship of price and marginal cost cannot be established.

8. When the economic performance of monopolistically competitive firms is compared with that of purely competitive firms, which one of the following is found to be true?
   a. In monopolistic competition, price is higher, output is greater, and unit cost is higher.
   b. In monopolistic competition, price is lower, output is greater, and unit cost is higher.
   c. In monopolistic competition, price is higher, output is lower, and unit cost is higher.
   d. In monopolistic competition, price is higher, output is lower, and unit cost is lower.

9. "The procedure of criticizing the economic performance of firms in monopolistic competition in comparison with those in pure competition may give misleading results." Which of the following comments most accurately on that statement?
   a. True; any results that the comparison might suggest are outweighed by the fact that monopolistic competition is more advantageous to an economy than other kinds of markets are, in that it leads to rapid development of technology.
   b. True; assuming that the cost curves are the same for firms in the two market situations is not realistic.
   c. False; one cannot criticize the practice of comparing the economic performance of firms in the two market situations.
   d. True; because both market situations are highly competitive and the differences in market performance may not be significant.

10. When one speaks of the "wastes" of monopolistic competition, one refers to the fact that
    a. Monopolistically competitive firms produce at less than economic capacity.
    b. In monopolistically competitive industries, air and water pollution is especially bad.
    c. In monopolistically competitive firms, management is notoriously inefficient.
    d. Actually, as the use of the quotation marks indicates, there are no wastes in monopolistic competition.

11. The "wastes" of monopolistic competition tend to be low due to the fact that
    a. Elasticity of demand tends to be low.
    b. Elasticity of demand tends to be high.
    c. Elasticity of demand is unity.
    d. The wastes are unrelated to the elasticity of demand.

Match the phrases in column B to the terms in column A.

Column A	Column B
1. Pure competition	(a) Only one firm
2. Pure monopoly	(b) Low point of long-run average cost
3. Monopolistic competition	(c) Homogeneous product
4. Homogeneous product	(d) Buyer believes there is a difference between output of different sellers
5. Differentiated product	(e) Price equals average cost
6. Wastes of monopolistic competition	(f) Produce at less than full capacity
7. Full capacity	(g) Differentiated product
8. Economic profit	(h) Price is above average total cost
9. Normal profit	(i) A characteristic of pure competition

ANSWERS

Part 4

Section A 1, T; 2, T; 3, F; 4, F; 5, F; 6, F; 7, T; 8, T; 9, T; 10, F; 11, T; 12, T; 13, F; 14, F

Section B 1, *d*; 2, *b*; 3, *c*; 4, *a*; 5, *a*; 6, *b*; 7, *a*; 8, *c*; 9, *d*; 10, *a*; *11, b*

Section C 1, c; 2, a; 3, g; 4, i; 5, d; 6, f; 7, b; 8, h; 9, c

CHAPTER 10   *Oligopoly: Imperfect Competition Among the Few*

PART 1

Reread the section entitled "Summing Up" at the end of Chapter 10. It offers an excellent review of the material in the chapter.

Things to Watch For

Chapter 10

Chapter 10 begins with a definition of **oligopoly**. The most important characteristic of oligopoly is **interdependency**. The actions of one firm affect the actions of all the others in the industry. This interdependence engenders as many different kinds of oligopoly behavior as there are different ways of firms' interacting.

Because of interdependence there are different ways firms can interact and thus different models of oligopoly behavior. Economists have identified three broad categories of oligopoly firms. Class I is called organized and collusive. Class II is unorganized and collusive. Class III is unorganized and non-collusive.

Class I (organized, collusive) behavior involves cooperation in price setting and other conditions of the market. Cartels or trusts are formed, an act which is illegal according to antitrust laws since the results are much like those of pure monopoly. The student here needs to understand the economic effects especially the dead weight losses identified through the concepts of consumers' and producers' surpluses.

An important form of class II (unorganized, collusive) oligopoly is price leadership. Again the student should be familiar with the price leader (dominant firm) presentation of the economic effects of price leadership including the dead weight losses.

An important example of class III or unorganized non-collusive oligopoly is kinked demand oligopoly.

In a *kinked-demand oligopoly*, the assumptions are that (1) if one firm *lowers* its prices, others follow suit, to protect themselves against losing customers; and (2) if one firm *raises* its prices, others do not follow suit, so that the first firm loses customers. This difference in the behaviors that follow an increase and a decrease in prices creates a kink or bend in the demand curve and a vertical or discontinuous section in the marginal-revenue curve.

This situation breeds inflexibility of prices. It does so for a number of reasons. (1) If a given firm raises its prices, its total revenue tends to decline. On the other hand, if it lowers prices, its competitors follow suit, and again the firm's total revenue tends to go down. (2) A price cut by one firm may initiate a price war. (3) Cost can vary somewhat without causing prices to change. In other words, the marginal-cost curve can shift within the gap or discontinuous area and not change price.

Price competition seldom occurs in an oligopoly, though various kinds of *non-price competition* do. These include (1) differences in styling, (2) differences in services offered, (3) differences in quality, and (4) advertising.

Perhaps the most important form of non-price competition is advertising. There are various justifications for advertising, as well as various criticisms of it. Bear in mind two points: (1) From the point of view of the consumer, the clear advantage of advertising is that it often gives information one needs for making intelligent choices. (2) Hardly anyone would want to see advertising eliminated altogether. Some people would, however, like to see certain abuses done away with.

We have been assuming that any firm produces at such a level of output—and sets the price of its product at such a level—as to maximize its profits. This assumption is probably valid in most cases. However, economists have pointed out six flaws in this theory, six reasons why the assumption may not be true. You should understand these arguments. However, do realize that these criticisms do not really refute the assumption that firms are profit-maximizing. They merely point out that establishing profit maximization is more complicated than meets the eye.

One argument, however, that comes closest to a refutation involves those firms whose decision-makers are not the owners of the firm. These managers may be more concerned with satisficing or seeking an acceptable level of profit. This may be so because in attempting to maximize the manager's returns and area of control they need to increase the size of the firm. Thus they concentrate on sales maximization rather than profit.

PART 2

Define the following terms and concepts.

1. Oligopoly
2. Interdependency
3. Kinked demand
4. Price leadership
5. Trust, cartel

6. Entry limit pricing
7. Satisficing
8. Sales Maximization hypothesis
9. Conscious parallelism

PART 3

Answer the following questions and problems.

1. What are the chief characteristics of oligopoly? Of what significance is interdependency when one is constructing a model of oligopoly behavior?

2. In Figure 10-1 are two sets of curves depicting demand and marginal revenue. Draw solid-line curves representing demand and marginal revenue for a situation in which there is kinked-demand oligopoly. When price declines from point A, which D and MR curve, 1 or 2, should be solid? When price increases from point A, which D and MR curve, 1 or 2, should be solid?

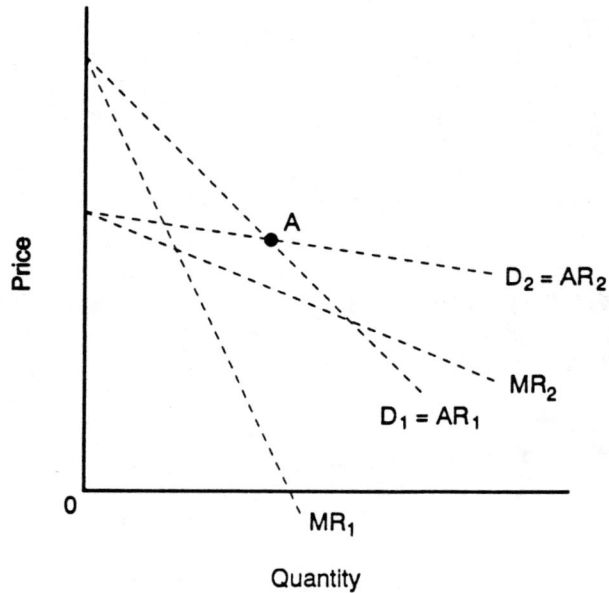

Figure 10-1 Graph for Problem 2

3. In Figure 10-2, redraw the kinked-demand-oligopoly curve for demand and marginal revenue and add the cost curves. Indicate the equilibrium price and quantity, and then shade in the rectangles showing total revenue, total cost, and economic profit. If you have any difficulties, refer to Figure 10-3 in the text.

4. Referring to your Figure 10-2, explain why price tends to be inflexible in the kinked-demand model.

5. Does it make any difference in terms of the probability of kinked-oligopoly behavior if prices increase mildly with plentiful supplies or increase sharply with short supplies?

6. What is meant by Class I oligopoly? Give illustrations.

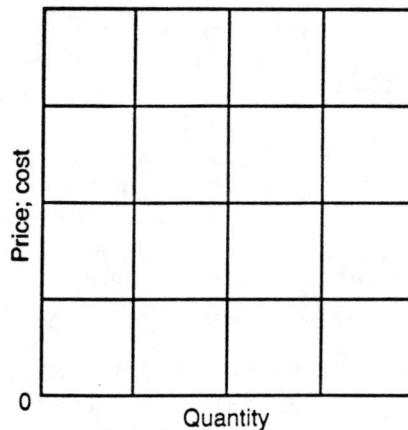

Figure 10-2 Graph for Problems 3 and 4

7. Why is price leadership not necessarily illegal? Draw and explain a diagram illustrating price leadership in a dominant firm-fringe firm industry.

8. Which do you think is more prevalent in oligopolistic industries: price competition or non-price competition? Why?

9. Discuss briefly the four kinds of non-price competition mentioned in the text. Which do you consider beneficial to the consumer? Why?

10. Enumerate the four ways in which some people claim advertising benefits the consumer. Then criticize these four points. In your opinion, is advertising worth its cost to society? Why?

11. Present the argument against the assumption that firms maximize their profits. Pay particular attention to sales maximizing behavior in your answer.

PART 4 Self-test

SECTION A True/false questions

T   F   1. In an oligopoly, interdependence among firms causes as many models of oligopoly as there are assumptions about how oligopolistic firms react to the actions of any one firm in the industry.

T   F   2. In the curves depicting the situation in a kinked-demand oligopoly, there is a sharp bend or kink at the prevailing price, because elasticity changes markedly as firms react differently to a price decrease as opposed to a price increase.

T   F   3. The model of the kinked-demand oligopoly shows that an individual firm in an oligopoly can obtain higher profits than a group of oligopolistic firms acting collusively because an individual firm can react quickly to changing conditions of demand and cost, while oligopolistic firms that are in collusion are restrained by the agreements they have made.

T   F   4. When there is price leadership in an oligopoly, the industry has an unwritten rule that all the firms in the industry will follow the pricing policy of one agreed-on leading firm.

T   F   5. In an oligopoly, price competition is not the rule; therefore, oligopolistic firms use various forms of non-price competition.

T   F   6. There is no argument about the statement that advertising benefits the consumer because it provides free TV and radio, and reduces prices of newspapers and magazines.

T   F   7. The arguments presented to refute the economists' assumption that all firms seek to maximize profits reveal that profit-maximizing behavior is a more complicated process to estimate than the assumption indicates.

T   F   8. In the soft drink industry, the lack of a dominant firm causes the market to behave as a purely competitive one.

T   F   9. Conscious parallelism does not exist in price leadership because price leadership is illegal according to the anti-trust laws.

T   F   10. Satisficing and sales maximization may occur in firms managed by people who do not own them. This tends to result in larger size and lower profits for such firms.

SECTION B Multiple-choice questions

1. The characteristic that is unique to oligopolistic firms—that is not present in firms that come under other market classifications—is
   a. homogeneous products.
   b. differentiated products.
   c. interdependence.
   d. advertising.
   e. barriers to entry.

2. The assumption on which the kinked-demand model of an oligopoly is based is that
   a. when one firm increases its price, other firms follow suit, but when one firm decreases its price, other firms do not follow suit.
   b. when one firm increases its price, other firms do not follow suit, but when one firm decreases its price, other firms do follow suit.
   c. other firms meet any price increase or decrease instituted by a given firm.
   d. other firms ignore both increases and decreases in price instituted by a given firm.

3. "In a kinked-demand oligopoly, prices tend toward inflexibility." Which one of the following statements does *not* support that conclusion?
   a. When one firm increases its prices, other firms do not follow suit, and the firm loses large numbers of customers to the other lower-priced firms.
   b. When one firm decreases its prices, other firms do follow suit, and the firm gains only small numbers of customers.
   c. When one firm decreases its prices, price wars may break out as other firms try to prevent the first firm from obtaining an advantage on account of having a lower price.
   d. As firms' costs vary, their marginal cost equals their marginal revenue at a different level of output but still at the same price.

4. Which of the following statements about price leadership is *not* true?
   a. The government provides the leadership through wage and price guidelines.
   b. Price leadership does not violate the antitrust laws.
   c. When it comes to prices, an industry follows the lead of certain firms.
   d. The price leader must set prices at such a level that the rest of the firms in the industry will achieve acceptable profits.

5. Which of the following is *not* a form of non-price competition?
   a. Variations in style
   b. Variations in services
   c. Variations in quality
   d. Advertising
   e. All of the above

6. Which one of the following is *not* a benefit claimed for advertising in the text?
   a. Because advertising increases demand, it may cause costs to fall on account of economies of scale more than it causes costs to increase on account of increased selling costs.
   b. Advertising increases firms' efficiency of production because it makes them compete with one another.
   c. Advertising provides information consumers need in order to make intelligent choices.
   d. Advertising provides free TV and radio to consumers.

7. The argument against the assumption that all firms seek mainly to maximize profits is supported by which one of the following statements?
   a. Oligopolistic and monopolistic firms would have a hard time computing realistic demand, marginal-revenue, and marginal-cost curves.
   b. Business people are often motivated by social concerns that lead to less-than-maximum profits.
   c. The technocrats who *really* make the decisions for the large corporations are motivated mainly by the desire to maintain control rather than the desire to maximize profits.
   d. All of the above statements tend to support arguments against the profit-maximizing assumption.

8. Price leadership in the steel industry caused which results?
   a. The price leader set prices at the competitive level to assure maximum efficiency.
   b. The price was such that no dead weight loss occured out of fear of government action.
   c. Price leadership exhibited some if not all the dead weight losses of monopoly.
   d. The fringe firms prices tended to be higher than in monopoly.

9. In reviewing the profit maximizing assumption which of the following is most correct?
   a. The profit maximizing process is more complicated than the model suggests.
   b. Sales maximization may take precedent over profit maximization in some corporations.
   c. Economists still widely employ the profit maximizing assumption despite the criticisms.
   d. All of the above are correct about the profit maximizing assumption.

SECTION C Matching questions

1. Match the phrases in column B to the terms in column A.

Column A	Column B
1. Oligopoly	(a) Illegal procedure
2. Kinked-demand oligopoly	(b) Tacit agreements by firms to follow the pricing policy of one firm in the industry
3. Class I oligopoly	(c) If the firm lowers its price, others follow suit, if the firm raises its price, others do not follow suit
4. Price leadership	(d) A few interdependent firms
5. Non-price competition	(e) Style, services, quality, and advertising

2. Indicate whether the phrase in column A fits pure competition (PC), monopolistic competition (MC), oligopoly (O), or pure monopoly (PM) by writing the appropriate abbreviations in column B. A phrase may fit more than one market classification.

Column A	Column B
1. Many small firms	_____
2. Homogeneous product	_____
3. Differentiated product	_____
4. Few firms	_____
5. Only one firm	_____
6. Complete barriers to entry	_____
7. Substantial barriers to entry	_____
8. Advertising	_____
9. Kink in demand	_____
10. Discontinuous section in marginal revenue	_____
11. D, AR, and MR are equal	_____
12. MR lies below D and AR	_____
13. Price equals marginal cost	_____
14. Interdependency	_____
15. Price lies above marginal cost	_____
16. Production at full capacity	_____
17. Only a normal profit in the long run	_____
18. Probability of normal profit in the long run	_____
19. Probability of economic profit in the long run	_____
20. Inefficient allocation of resources	_____

ANSWERS

Part 4

Section A   1, T; 2, T; 3, F; 4, T; 5, T; 6, F; 7, T; 8, F; 9, F; 10, T

Section B   1, *c*; 2, *b*; 3, *d*; 4, *a*; 5, *e*; 6, *b*; 7, *d*; 8, *c*; 9, *d*

Section C   I.   1, d; 2, c; 3, a; 4, b; 5, e

                II.   1, PC, MC; 2, PC, O; 3, MC, O; 4, O; 5, PM; 6, PM; 7, O; 8, MC, O, PM; 9, O; 10, O; 11, PC; 12, MC, O, PM; 13, PC; 14, O; 15, MC, O, PM; 16, PC; 17, PC 18, MC; 19, O, PM; 20, MC, O, PM

CHAPTER 11   *The Factor Markets: Not Only Products are Sold*

Application 11   *How Much Education Should We Buy?*

PART 1

Reread the sections entitled "Summing Up" at the end of Chapter 11 and Application 11. These sections provide an excellent review of the chapter and the application.

Things to Watch For

Chapter 11

Chapter 11 treats the other side of the market system—the **factor markets**, or markets in which resources are allocated (that is, bought and sold). Individuals and firms obtain all their market incomes (rent, interest, profits, wages) from the operation of this system of markets. And the prices of factors, like the prices of products, are established by supply and demand.

Demand for a factor is a **derived demand**. That is, it is created by and dependent on the expected demand for products produced by the factor. Only a change in the price of a factor can cause a change in the quantity of that factor demanded by firms. Demand for a factor may be changed by (1) the amount of demand for the product produced by the factor, (2) the productivity of the factor [which is in turn influenced by (a) productivity of the resource, (b) technology, (c) managerial ability, and (d) productivity of other resources], and (3) prices of other factors of production.

A firm will hire enough resources to produce at its most profitable rate of output (MR = MC). The firm will hire any given factor up to the point at which the factor contributes no more to revenue than to cost—that is, no more to profit.

Let us assume that labor is the variable input. A competitive employer, one who can't affect the going wage or the price at which the firm's product is sold, will hire labor up to the point at which the constant average wage is equal to labor's **value of marginal product**, VMP (marginal physical product times price of the product the labor produces). If the firm hired more than the amount of labor that makes the wage equal to VMP, then labor would add more to cost than to revenue (assuming diminishing marginal productivity). And to hire less than this amount of labor would mean that the firm would make less than the maximum profit (produce output at less than the most profitable level).

The key to this explanation of factor employment is the **law of variable proportions**.(diminishing returns). As a firm uses successive increments of a variable input in conjunction with a fixed input, the additions to output attributable to the variable input will diminish beyond some point. The key to this law is the assumption that the **marginal**

physical product of a resource—the additional output produced by an additional unit of resource—will diminish beyond some point.

For the competitive firm, the VMP of a resource is the same as the **marginal revenue product**, MRP which is the contribution that an additional unit of resources makes to total revenue. Thus a profit-maximizing competitive firm will hire resources until the price of those resources (labor's wage, for example) is equal to the VMP and MRP of the resources. Another way to say this is that the competitive firm's demand curve for a resource (actually, its derived-demand curve) is the same as the VMP and MRP curve for that resource.

To minimize the cost of producing at any particular rate of output, a firm will combine resources in such a way that a dollar spent on one kind of input yields the same amount of output as a dollar spent on any other. This can be represented by the following equation, where L = labor, K = capital, MPP_L = marginal physical product of labor, and MPP_K = marginal physical product of capital:

$$\frac{MPP_L}{P_L} = \frac{MPP_K}{P_K}.$$

To this rule, let us add another: The profit-maximizing rate of output is the rate at which **marginal resource cost**—the additional cost of a unit of resource (such as labor)—is equal to the marginal revenue product of that unit, or

$$MRC_L = MRP_L.$$

One can find the amount of a resource demanded by a whole industry by adding up the amounts demanded by all the firms at each possible price of the resource. This is true unless there are **resource externalities**, or changes in the costs of resources that are not attributable to the actions of firms. For example, if an industry increases output and, as a result, resource prices are bid up, then one can determine industry supply only by taking these externalities into account.

The **elasticity of resource demand** is the rate at which the quantity of a resource demanded changes as its price changes. This rate depends on four factors: (1) the rate at which the MPP of the factor declines (negagtive relationship), (2) the price elasticity of demand for the final product that the factor is used to produce (positive relationship), (3) the proportion of the total production cost represented by the factor (positively related), and (4) the degree of substitutability of the factor (positive relationship).

It is difficult (if not impossible) to relate the distribution of income that comes about as a result of paying resources competitively (paying them their VMP) to a "fair" distribution of income. This is so for several reasons. (1) The productivities of resources are *inter*dependent, and the degree of this interdependence is hard to measure. (2) There is no uniquely "fair" distribution of income. Besides, the fact that much of our market system is not competitive makes the issue a moot one. Furthermore, the theory of marginal productivity offers no insights into equity or justice.

If a firm or industry become monopolistic in its product market, it becomes unprofitable for the firm to hire as much of a resource as a competitive firm or industry does. What has happened is that the MRP of a given resource is no longer the same as its VMP. Marginal physical product remains the same (by assumption), but now the firm faces a downward-sloping demand curve for its product. To sell more output, the firm must lower its prices. Thus the marginal revenue contributed by an additional unit of resource (the MRP) is less than the marginal physical product times the constant selling price, that is, the price those units of output would bring under competitive conditions. Therefore, for a monopoly,

$$MRP < VMP.$$

The monopolistic firm (even though it hires resources competitively) produces less and hires fewer units of resources than the purely competitive firm, unless economies of scale is taken into consideration.

Application 11

Recently people have begun to question whether we are over investing in education. Economists view investment in education as investment in **human capital**, the improvement in human skills attributable to education. The "correct" amount of investment in education is the one at which the social return on investment in human capital is the same as the return on other types of social investment.

The social costs of education are (1) costs borne by students, (2) costs borne by the public, and (3) the opportunity costs of education (that is, the difference between a person's later, higher income and the income that person had to give up during schooling). The social benefits of education are (1) the higher lifetime earnings a person with greater education can expect, (2) the satisfaction that education gives the consumer, and (3) external benefits to society such as less crime.

As we do with any investment, we discount both these costs and these benefits back to the present. The problem is that there are three potentially different estimates of both. On the one hand, there are the estimates students make of the value they place on their education. Then there are parents' estimates. Then the public's (that is, the government's). Students pay little of the direct costs, so to them the benefits seem always to outweigh the costs. The returns to parents from children's education are largely psychic, so the rates of return to parents are hard to estimate. According to various studies, the **private rates of return**, those that do not take into account indirect private costs and external benefits, are indeed large—from 10 percent to 35 percent for various types of outlays. Age-earnings profiles show that earnings rise with education and that earnings rise with age (to 70). Whether education raises marginal productivity is not certain; one idea is that employers pay higher wages to better educated employees because the education is a signal to them about desirable attributes (time, orientation, etc.)

What about the public's return on its expenditures for higher education? Presumably, the public should spend enough on education to exhaust the externalities and to ensure that the nation's citizens produce and consume the socially "correct" amount of education.

The following is a list of the arguments that have been presented in favor of public subsidy of education. (1) There are imperfections in the capital markets. Students can't borrow the money to buy an education. (2) Subsidies to education redistribute income. (Neither of these first two arguments convinces most economists, and neither incorporates externalities.) (3) Subsidies to education bring about economic growth. (4) Subsidies to education reduce crime rates. (5) Subsidies to education improve the learning environment. (6) Educated people are better citizens than uneducated ones. (7) Education helps people to attain career orientation. (8) When citizens are educated, tax returns are higher and transfer payments lower.

PART 2

Define the following terms and concepts.

1. Factor markets
2. Derived demand
3. Marginal revenue productivity
4. Law of diminishing returns or variable proportions
5. Marginal revenue product
6. Value of marginal product
7. Marginal resource cost

8. Resource externalities
9. Elasticity of resource demand
10. Human capital
11. Private rates of return
12. Externalities of education
13. Age-earnings profile
14. Signaling`

PART 3

Answer the following questions and problems.

1. What income(s) do you derive from the factor market(s)? Do these markets seem *competitive* to you? Why?

2. Evaluate the statement that "an increase in the wage won't change the demand for labor."

3. Consider the data in Table 11-1 on demand for labor by a competitive grocery store (it sells competitively and hires labor competitively).
   a. Calculate the marginal revenue product and the value of marginal product of labor (column 6).
   b. How many units of labor will the firm hire if the competitive wage is $25 per day? $50 per day?

4. Consider Figure 11-1, which deals with the competitive employment of labor.
   a. What is the firm's demand curve for labor?
   b. Why does the demand curve for labor slope downward?
   c. How much labor will the firm employ if the wage is w_0? if it is w_1? Indicate these employment rates on the employment axis.
   d. Explain why the firm will find it most profitable to hire the amounts of labor you indicated in part c.

5. Why is the general rule

$$\frac{MPP_1}{P_1} = \frac{MPP_2}{P_2}$$

the least-cost way for a firm to combine resources 1 and 2?

6. How likely is it that there will be no resource externalities for an entire industry?

7. Is the distribution of income that comes about when there are competitive product and factor markets "fair"? What problems do you encounter in trying to answer this question?

Table 11-1 Competitive Hiring of Labor

1	2	3	4	5	6
Units of Variable Resource (L = labor)	Total Product (TP = output per day in hundreds)	Marginal Physical Product (MPP$_L$)	Product Price (P$_g$)	Total Revenue (TP x P$_g$)	Marginal Revenue Product (MRP = MPP$_L$ x P$_g$ = VMP)
0	0		$5	0	
		50			$
1	50		5	250	
		40			
2	90		5	450	
		30			
3	120		5	600	
		20			
4	140		5	700	
		10			
5	150		5	750	
		5			
6	155		5	775	
		3			
7	158		5	790	
		2			
8	160		5	800	
		1			
9	161		5	805	
		0			
10	161		5	805	

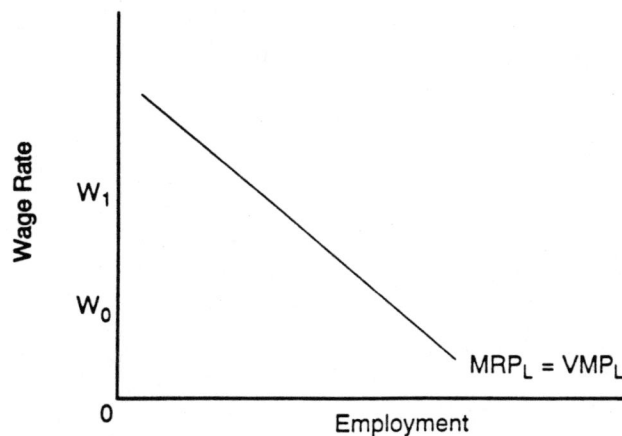

Figure 11-1 Competitive Employment

8. Consider the data on demand for monopolistic hiring of labor in Table 11-2.
   a. Calculate the marginal revenue product of labor (column 6).
   b. How many units of labor will the firm hire if the competitive wage is $54? $96?

9. Consider Figure 11-2, which deals with the hiring of labor by a monopolistic firm (which pays a competitive wage).
   a. What is the monopolistic firm's demand curve for labor? What would the curve be if the firm's product market became competitive?

b. Why does the firm's demand curve for labor slope downward?
c. How much labor will the firm hire if the wage is W_0? if it is W_1? Indicate these rates on the employment axis.
d. Explain why the firm will find it most profitable to hire the amounts of labor you indicated in part c.
e. Does this firm exploit labor? If so, in what sense? Indicate on the graph the amount of this exploitation at wages W_0 and W_1.

Table 11-2 Monopolistic Hiring of Labor

1	2	3	4	5	6
Units of Variable Resource (L)	Total Product Per Day (TP)	Marginal Physical Product (MPP_L)	Product Price (P_g)	Total Revenue ($TP \times P_g$)	Marginal Revenue Product ($MRP = MPP_L \times MR$)
0	0		$6.00	0	
		50			$
1	50		5.00	250.00	
		40			
2	90		4.00	360.00	
		30			
3	120		3.80	456.00	
		20			
4	140		3.60	504.00	
		10			
5	150		3.50	525.00	
		5			
6	155		3.40	527.00	
		3			
7	158		3.30	521.40	
		2			
8	160		3.20	512.00	
		1			
9	161		3.10	499.10	
		0			
10	161		3.10	499.10	

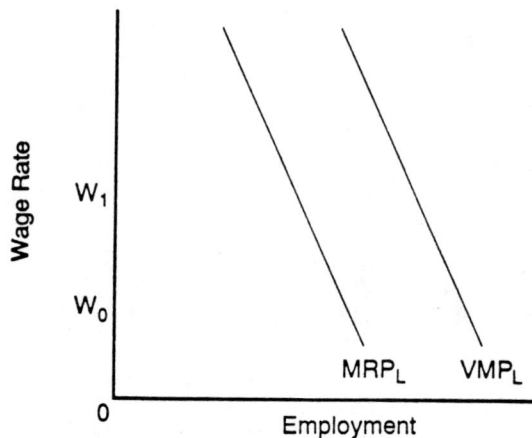

Figure 11-2 Employment by MonopolisticSeller Who Hires at a Competitive Wage

10. What do economists mean by the term *human capital*?

11. What is the "correct" amount for society to invest in any activity?

12. What problems do we encounter when we try to ensure that we are investing the "correct" amounts in education? In view of these problems, does it seem likely to you that we are investing the correct amounts?

13. What are the external benefits of education?

14. What does signaling have to do with wage payments and levels of education?

PART 4 Self-test

SECTION A True/false questions

T   F   1. Factor markets have little to do with the distribution of income.

T   F   2. The demand for factors is derived from the demand for final products.

T   F   3. The productivity of resources is greatly influenced by technology.

T   F   4. Technological unemployment has little to do with the relative rates at which the costs of wages and of capital change.

T   F   5. An employer who is a competitive producer will hire enough labor to make the wage paid to labor equal to the VMP of labor.

T   F   6. A firm that is a monopolistic producer and pays competitive wages will hire enough labor to make the wage paid to labor equal to the VMP of labor.

T   F   7. Value of marginal product and marginal revenue product are always equal.

T   F   8. In a competitive factor market situation, marginal resource cost is the same as the wage rate.

T   F   9. To minimize the cost of producing a particular rate of output, firms should make the MPPs of resources equal.

T   F   10. Resource externalities result from the actions of a single firm.

T   F   11. It is clear that we in the United States are investing too little in education.

T   F   12. The "correct" amount of social investment in education is the amount that makes the social return on investment in human capital equal to the private return on investment in education.

T   F   13. Private rates of return on investment in education are large.

T   F   14. Rates of return on investment in education hold steady regardless of the amount of this investment.

T   F   15. Age-earnings profiles indicate that wages rise with age and education only to age 50.

SECTION B Multiple-choice questions

1. Which one of the following does *not* determine changes in the demand for a factor of production?
   a. Demand for the final product.
   b. Price of that factor.
   c. Productivity of the resource.
   d. Prices of other factors.

2. The productivity of a resource is influenced by all but which one of the following?
   a. Resource prices.
   b. Technology.
   c. Managerial ability.
   d. Productivity of other resources.

3. One can define the law of diminishing returns or variable proportions in terms of which one of the following?
   a. Long-run period.
   b. Market period.
   c. Historical period.
   d. Short-run period.

4. The competitive firm's equilibrium employment situation is described by the relationship:
   a. $MR = MC$.
   b. $MC_L = MRC_L = P_L = S_L$.
   c. $MRP_L = VMP_L$.
   d. $MRP_L > VMP_L$.

5. The cost-minimizing rule for a firm is:
   a. $MPP_1/P_1 > MPP_2/P_2$.
   b. $MPP_1/P_1 = MPP_2/P_2$.
   c. $MPP_1/P_1 < MPP_2/P_2$.
   d. $\dfrac{MPP_K}{P_K} = \dfrac{MPP_L}{P_L}$.

6. The elasticity of demand for a resource is determined by all but which one of the following?
   a. Rate at which its MPP decreases.
   b. Price elasticity of demand for the final product it produces.
   c. Its price.
   d. Its substitutability for other factors.

7. A "just" distribution of income is hard to define because:
   a. Economists are not concerned about it.
   b. There aren't enough data.
   c. People don't like to talk about justice.
   d. What is "just" is not unique to a particular distribution of income.

8. The difficulty in establishing the correct amount of social investment in education is that:
   a. we don't have the necessary data.
   b. we don't know how to measure investment in education.
   c. we don't know how to measure the benefits of education.
   d. parents, students, and governments assess costs and benefits differently.

9. Which of the following arguments in favor of public subsidy of higher education does *not* involve externalities?
   a. Higher education redistributes income.
   b. Higher education leads to better citizenship.
   c. Higher education brings about economic growth.
   d. Higher education makes possible career orientation.

10. Which one of the following arguments for public subsidy of education do economists *not* generally accept?
   a. Subsidization of education brings about a reduction in the crime rate.
   b. Subsidizing education improves the learning environment.
   c. Higher education leads to higher tax returns and lower transfer payments.
   d. There are imperfections in the capital markets.

SECTION C Matching questions

Match the phrases in column B to the terms in column A.

Column A	Column B
1. Value of marginal product	(a) Rent, interest, wages, profits
2. Cost minimization	(b) Change in total revenue due to a change in resource usage
3. Resource externalities	
4. Elasticity of demand for resources	(c) Employers hire enough labor to make this equal to the competitive wage
5. Market incomes	
6. Technological unemployment	(d) Marginal physical product per dollar equal for all resources
7. Human capital	
8. Marginal revenue product	(e) Not attributable to the actions of one firm
9. Private rates of return	(f) Quantity of a resource demanded changes as price of the resource changes
10. Law of diminishing returns	
11. Signaling	(g) Wages rise more rapidly than capital costs
	(h) Applies only in the short run
	(i) Improvement in labor skills
	(j) Do not include indirect social costs and external benefits.
	(k) Employers regard education as evidence of desirable traits

ANSWERS

PART 4

Section A 1, F; 2, T; 3, T; 4, F; 5, T; 6, F; 7, F; 8, T; 9, F; 10, F 11, F; 12, F; 13, T;
14, F; 15, F

Section B 1, *b*; 2, *a*; 3, *d*; 4, *b*; 5, *d*; 6, *c*; 7, *d*; 8, *d*; 9, *a*; 10, *d*

Section C 1, c; 2, d; 3, e; 4, f; 5, a; 6, g; 7, i; 8, b; 9, j; 10, h; 11, k

CHAPTER 12 *How Wage Rates and Other Factor Prices Are Set*

PART 1

Reread the section entitled "Summing Up" at the end of Chapter 12 It provides an excellent review of the material in the chapter.

Things to Watch For

Chapter 12

Chapter 12 deals with how the prices of factors (wages, rents, interest, and profits) are established. On the subject of *wages*, the chapter assumes that the quantity of labor supplied increases as the wage rate rises. That is, the supply curve for labor slopes upward. However, the supply curve of an individual worker may bend backward as the tradeoff between having more income (the income effect of a wage increase) and having more leisure (the substitution effect of a wage increase) changes. Since the wage at which this may occur is not the same for all individuals (tradeoffs are different for different people), the market supply of labor is upward-sloping.

There are many wage rates. People differ in their skills and abilities, for reasons that are partly innate and partly a function of differences in education and training. However, it is the elasticity of resource supply—the rate at which the quantity supplied changes with an increased wage (or salary)—that influences the payment to a factor. *For a given demand condition, the less elastic the supply, the greater the wage.*

Then how do we account for the fact that people with the same skills get paid different wages? (1) Wage and job discrimination. Some employers decline to hire members of certain racial or ethnic groups or, if they do hire them, do not pay them on the basis of their productivity. (2) Nonmonetary considerations. (3) Immobility of labor.

The independent influences of supply and demand set a competitive wage. A competitive wage is a market-clearing wage. In other words, it is a wage that eliminates excess demand or supply of labor, or that makes quantity demanded equal to quantity supplied. No single firm in a competitive situation can influence this wage. But each firm responds to it and, in doing so, hires enough labor to make the wage equal to the VMP of labor. The wage is the firm's marginal resource cost. If the firm is a monopolistic product seller, it hires enough labor to make the wage equal to the MRP of labor. Since MRP < VMP to the monopolistic firm, it hires less labor than the purely competitive one.

A noncompetitive labor market may come about because (1) a **monopsony** exists; there is only one buyer of labor; (2) the labor supply is monopolistic (due to unions); and (3) the government creates noncompetitive conditions, for example, by setting minimum-wage laws.

A monopsonistic firm faces the entire upward-sloping labor supply. Thus, if the firm wants to hire more labor, it must pay a higher wage. This means that the firm's marginal resource cost (its MRC) becomes greater than the wage (since a particular wage applies to all units of labor employed). The firm that is monopsonistic with respect to hiring labor and monopolistic when it comes to selling its product must operate in such a way that its MRC is equal to its MRP Therefore, the result of monopsony is that the level of employment declines and wages become lower than the wages paid by firms that hire labor competitively and that have a monopoly on their products. In a monopsonistic situation, labor is paid less than its MRP. This differenceis called **technical factor exploitation**.

If a labor supply monopoly (a union) enters the picture, the situation becomes one of *bilateral monopoly*—two monopolies confonting each other. The wage that results will be somewhere between the wage the firm would prefer to pay (the equilibrium wage at the most profitable output for the firm) and the wage the union would prefer to get (the MRP of labor at the firm's profit-maximizing rate of output). What the wage will be depends on the relative bargaining strength of labor and management.

The effect of government-decreed minimum wages is usually to raise the wage of those who are employed but to reduce the level of employment. The minimum wage becomes the MRC for the firm. But since it is above the marginal-revenue productivity of many workers previously employed at the market wage, unemployment results. Governments may set wages, but they cannot legislate market incomes.

Chapter 12 also deals with economic discrimination as it applies to jobs and wages. **Job discrimination** exists when firms hire employees on the basis of considerations other than productivity, considerations such as race, color, or sex. **Wage discrimination** exists when firms hire workers on an equal basis but don't pay them strictly on the basis of their productivity. The **crowding theory** is the theory that blacks, women, and others are pushed into some jobs and out of others. People use the crowding theory to explain why wages and incomes are lower for racial minorities and women than for white males. When an employer pays unequal wages to those who are doing the same work, the explanation given is that there are certain employer "tastes for discrimination." That is, the demand schedules for female workers and minority workers are different from the demand schedules for male, white workers. The result is that income is skewed in favor of white males. This is a form of factor exploitation in which women and racial minorities receive lower wages than white males even if they are employed on the basis of their productivities. **Customer discrimination**—buyers' tastes for discrimination—seems to contribute as much to this factor exploitation as employers' tastes for discrimination.

Discrimination can be dealt with by (1) public action (such as civil rights laws), and (2) private action. If people refuse to buy the products of firms that practice discrimination, these firms lose the profits they get from discrimination. This would represent one form of private action. Also there is union pressure against discrimination. Another way to neutralize discrimination is to help members of minority groups to become entrepreneurs.

On the subject of *rents*, Chapter 12 begins with the fact that the total supply of land is inelastic. The payment to *any* resource that is in perfectly inelastic supply is called **economic rent**. Demand determines the price of any such resource. As demand increases, the price of the resource goes up correspondingly. Do land rents, like other prices, serve as useful signals of the efficiency with which the resource is being used? In the aggregate, no; a change in rents cannot change the supply of land. But in individual cases, yes, since the relative size of rents may indicate how land can be used most efficiently (office buildings versus farms, and so on). However, many resources or goods are not perfectly inelastic but are relatively inelastic in supply. In these cases, **Quasi-rents**, the differences between the actual payment to a resource and its opportunity costs, exist.

The single-tax movement was a movement toward taxing away all rents on land. No doubt this could be done, but there are weaknesses in the idea. (1) It's hard to separate returns that come from rent from returns that accrue from capital investment and the labor employed on the lands. (2) Relative land rents *do* serve as useful signals of the efficiency of use of the land resource. (3) Who is to say that rents are unearned but capital gains are earned? (4) The revenue the government would get from land-rent taxes would be small in relation to the cost of modern government.

Chapter 12 next takes up the subject of *interest*. Capital takes the form of **physical capital** (plant and equipment) and **financial capital** (flows of investment funds). The price of capital is the interest rate. The quantity of capital supplied increases as the interest rate increases. The quantity of capital demanded increases as the interest rate falls. (Firms borrow enough to make the MRP of capital equal to the interest rate R_K, where R stands for rate and K for capital. As R_K falls, firms borrow more.) Interest rates vary because of differences in (1) risk, (2) the degree of liquidity of the loan, (3) the length of the loan, and (4) the competitiveness of capital markets.

Interest rates in Canada are greatly influenced by government intervention in financial capital markets. This is because interest rates not only ration the supply of capital, but also affect investment, growth, and employment, subjects that governments consider too important to trust to chance movements of the capital market.

Also, Chapter 12 deals with **profit**. Profit is the return to entrepreneurs who take the risks involved in organizing resources into firms that produce goods and services. An **economic profit** is a return above the entrepreneur's opportunity cost. There are three interrelated theories of economic profit. (1) When a firm has **monopoly power**, barriers to entry make it possible for the firm to make an economic profit. (2) When a firm makes **innovations**, economic profit is a return on the introduction of new products and processes. This return will disappear when supplies of the product increase as there are further innovators. (3) When risk and uncertainty are high, the firm could encounter either profits or losses. When profits serve as signals to other firms to introduce technological change and improve their organization, economists say that the profits are *earned*.

PART 2

Define the following terms and concepts.

1. Resource supply
2. Backward-bending supply
3. Elasticity of resource supply
4. Economic discrimination
5. Wage discrimination
6. Job discrimination
7. Monopsony
8. Unions
9. Closed Shop
10. Economic rent
11. Single-tax movement
12. Relative rent
13. Physical capital
14. Financial capital
15. Entrepreneurship
16. Risk
17. Uncertainty
18. Surplus value
19. Crowding theory
20. Technical factor exploitation
21. Quasi-rents or common rents
22. Featherbedding
23. Comparable worth

PART 3

Answer the following questions and problems.

1. Why is it reasonable to suppose that the curves depicting the supply of labor will slope upward? Why do people supply more labor time at relatively higher wages than at relatively lower wages?

2. Consider Figure 12-1, and then answer the following questions.
    a. What do economists call the labor supply curve in Figure 12-1?
    b. What causes it to have the shape it does?
    c. Would you expect this to be the shape of the labor supply curves for all individuals? of your own labor supply curve? Why?
    d. Would you expect the bend to be at the same wage for all individuals (at W_0 in the figure)? Why?

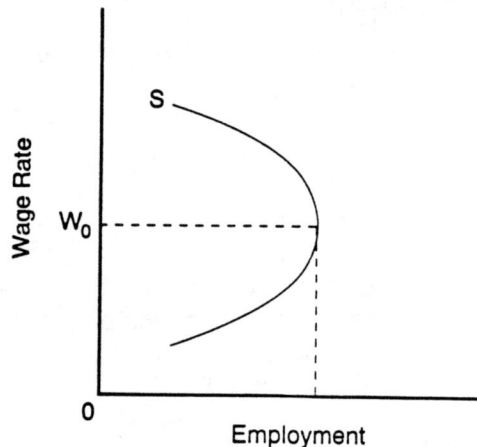

Figure 12-1 Labor Supply

3. What causes people with the same skills to be paid different wages? What causes people with different skills to be paid different wages?

4. How are the behavior of the Canadian Medical Association and the behavior of trade unions alike when these organizations act to increase the payments to their members?

5. Consider Figure 12-2, which deals with competitive employment. Then answer the following questions.
    a. What is the equilibrium competitive wage? What is the equilibrium level of employment? (Indicate this on the employment axis.)
    b. How much labor will the firm employ if it is a competitive product seller? a monopolistic product seller? (Indicate each on the employment axis of the firm.)
    c. Why did the level of employment fall when labor was hired by a monopolistic product seller?

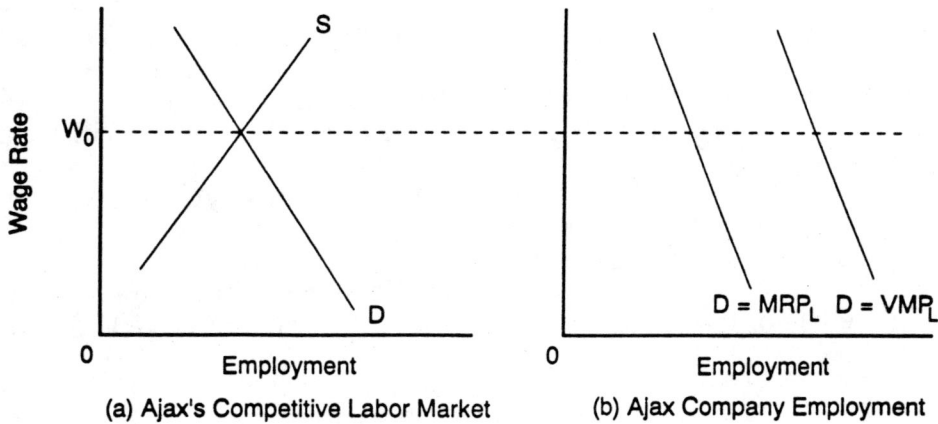

Figure 12-2 Competitive Employment, Ajax Company

6. Use Figure 12-3, which deals with monopsonistic hiring, to answer the questions that follow.
   a. Why is the marginal resource cost of labor (MRC_L) above the supply of labor (S_L)?
   b. What will the equilibrium wage rate and the employment rate be if the monopsonistic employer is a *competitive* product seller? What distance measure technical factor exploitation at this employment rate?
   c. What will the equilibrium wage rate and the employment rate be if the monopsonistic employer is a *monopolistic* product seller? What distance measures technical factor exploitation at this employment rate?
   d. Suppose that the Ajax Company, a monopsonistic firm, is confronted by the Ajax Workers Union. (This would be a bilateral monopoly.) (1) What level of employment would result? (2) Within what range would the wage rate be? What wage would labor prefer? What wage would management prefer? (3) What would determine the wage eventually settled on?

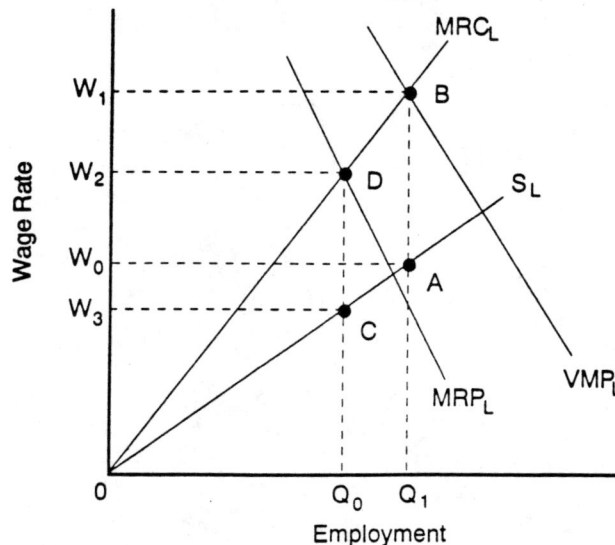

Figure 12-3 Monopsonistic Hiring, Ajax Company

7. Consider Figure 12-4, which deals with minimum wages. Then answer the following questions.
   a. What is the equilibrium wage rate before a minimum wage is imposed?
   b. If the government sets the minimum wage at $3.50, what will happen to the level of employment?
   c. What causes the level of employment to change when the government sets a minimum wage?
   d. Who are better off and who are worse off as a result of the $3.50 minimum wage?
   e. What does the figure suggest about the likelihood of a government's improving the welfare of low-income people by passing minimum-wage legislation?

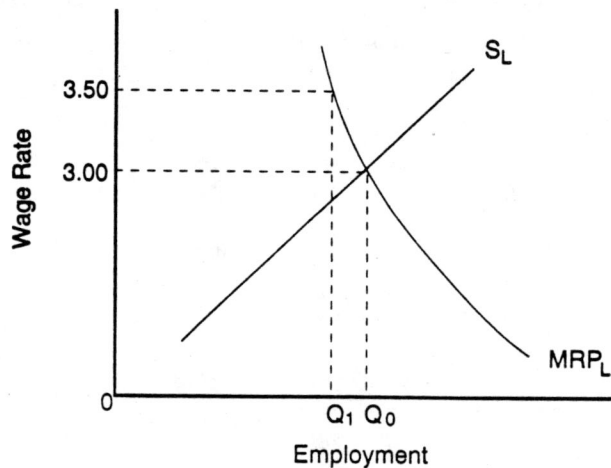

Figure 12-4 Effects of Minimum Wages

8. Consider Figure 12-5, which deals with economic rent. Then answer the following questions.
   a. What is the elasticity of supply of land in Figure 12-5?
   b. What is the rent on land, given that the demand for it is D_0? What kind of good is land under this condition?

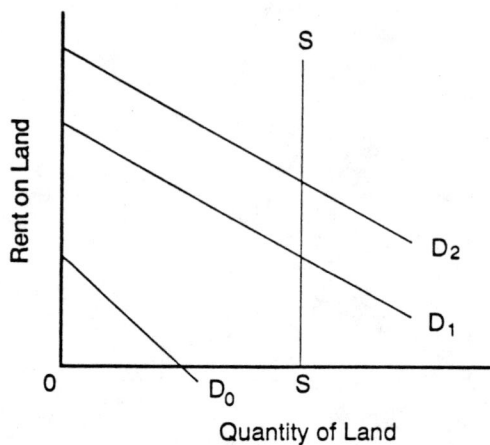

Figure 12-5 Determining Land Rents

c. What happens to land rent if population and income grow and demand increases to D_1? to D_2? What, then, determines land rents?

d. Could all the rent at demand D_1 be taxed away without changing the supply of land? What problems would arise if this were done?

9. Consider Figure 12-6, which deals with how interest rates are determined. Then answer the following questions.

a. Why does the curve depicting demand for loanable funds slope downward?

b. Why does the curve depicting supply of loanable funds slope upward?

c. What is the equilibrium interest rate?

d. Suppose the government thought the interest rate was too high (for reasons having to do with investment, growth, or employment). How could the government cause the rate to be reduced?

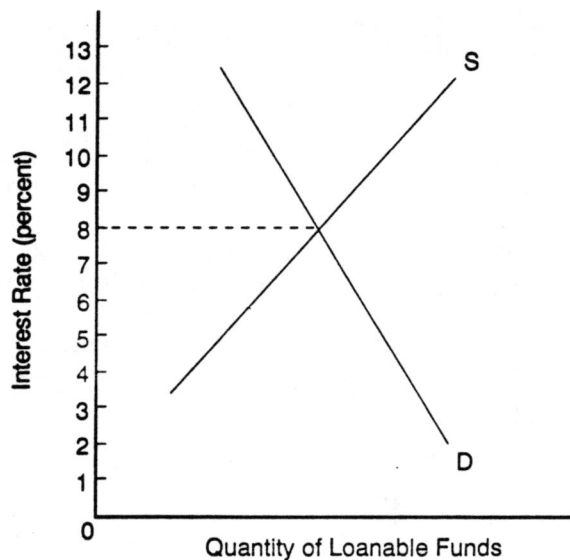

Figure 12-6 Determining Interest Rates

10. What theories do economists advance to explain the existence of *economic profit*? Can one say that economic profit is earned? Why or why not?

11. What effects does the crowding of women and minorities into certain jobs and out of others have on

a. relative wages of white men compared with women and minorities?

b. relative incomes of these two groups?

12. What effects do "tastes for discrimination" (either by an employer or by the employer's customers) have on relative wages and incomes of white men, on the one hand, and women and minorities, on the other?

13. Do crowding and "tastes for discrimination" have the same effects on productivity as on wages and incomes? Why?

PART 4 Self-test

SECTION A True/false questions

T   F   1. The supply of a resource is the relation between the price of a resource and the supply of it.

T   F   2. The supply curve for the total labor supply is just as likely to be a backward-bending one as the supply curve for an individual worker.

T   F   3. Elasticity of labor supply explains part of the difference between wage rates for attorneys and those for secretaries.

T   F   4. The less elastic the supply of a resource, the higher its wage (for a given demand condition) and the less the technical factor exploitation.

T   F   5. Nonmonetary considerations have nothing to do with economic decisions.

T   F   6. A competitive employer will hire labor up to the point at which the wage paid to labor is equal to labor's value of marginal product.

T   F   7. A noncompetitive (monopolistic) employer will hire labor up to the point at which the wage paid to labor is equal to labor's marginal revenue product.

T   F   8. Technical factor exploitation refers to the failure of employers to pay a just wage to their workers.

T   F   9. When the government sets minimum wages, this is likely to increase employment in competitive labor markets.

T   F   10. A monopsonistic employer will hire as much labor as a competitive employer.

T   F   11. In a bilateral monopoly, for a given rate of employment, the wage eventually agreed on will be between labor's MRP and its supply-determined price.

T   F   12. One cannot tax away economic rents without affecting the supply of land.

T   F   13. Demand is what determines economic rents.

T   F   14. One cannot consider rent to be a useful market signal.

T   F   15. The more elastic the supply of a resource, the greater the quasi-rent.

T   F   16. The price of capital is so important that governments are unlikely to let it seek just any level determined by the market.

T   F   17. Economists agree that economic profits are always unearned.

T   F   18. In a business situation involving uncertainty, economic profits are possible but losses cannot occur.

T   F   19. Job discrimination and wage discrimination have the same effects.

T   F   20. Even if present discriminatory practices were ended, discrimination would still exist.

T   F   21. The crowding theory helps to explain why people doing the same jobs are not always paid the same wages.

T   F   22. All discrimination is attributable to employers.

T   F   23. Some economists believe that competitive pressures can eliminate much job and wage discrimination.

T   F   24. It is clear that the income gap between men and women is closing completely and quickly.

SECTION B Multiple-choice questions

1. Total labor supplied increases as wages increase because of all but which one of the following?
   a. People prefer higher incomes to lower ones.
   b. The amount of leisure people desire differs from one person to the next.
   c. Wages are always competitively set.
   d. The Puritan ethic remains strong.

2. All but which one of the following reasons help to explain the existence of many different wage scales?
   a. Wage discrimination exists.
   b. Skills differ from one person to the next.
   c. Elasticities of the labor supply differ.
   d. Supplies of the resource (labor) are perfectly elastic.

3. People with similar skills receive different wages because of all but one of the following. Which?
   a. Immobility of the resource (labor)
   b. Economic discrimination
   c. Minimum wage laws
   d. Nonmonetary considerations

4. A competitive employer will hire labor up to the point at which the wage paid to labor is equal to
   a. VMP_L.
   b. MPP_L.
   c. MPP_L/P_L.
   d. MR.

5. A noncompetitive employer will hire labor up to the point at which the wage paid to labor is equal to
   a. VMP_L.
   b. MRP_L.
   c. MRC_L.
   d. MPP_L.

6. All but which one of the following may introduce noncompetitive conditions into labor markets?
   a. Minimum wage laws
   b. Unions
   c. A monopsonistic firm
   d. A change in MPP_L

7. The most profitable rate of employment for a monopsonistic firm that holds a monopoly on the product it produces is the rate at which
   a. $S_L = VMP_L$.
   b. $MRC_L = MRP_L$.
   c. $MRC_L = S_L$.
   d. $VMP_L = MRP_L$.

8. In a bilateral monopoly, the wage that is eventually decided on will be a wage somewhere between
   a. MRC_L and S_L.
   b. VMP_L and S_L.
   c. MRP_L and MRC_L.
   d. VMP_L and MRP_L.

9. Technical factor exploitation occurs under which of the following conditions.
   a. Competitive demand for labor
   b. Competitve supply of labor
   c. Monopsonistic demand for labor
   d. Monopolistic supply of labor

10. When the price of a resource is greater than its opportunity cost the difference is called
    a. Economic rent
    b. Quasi-rent
    c. Economic profit
    d. Normal profit

11. All but which one of the following help to explain why economic rent on land exists?
    a. There is only so much land.
    b. Land is nonreproducible
    c. Land has alternative uses.
    d. Land is in relatively elastic supply.

12. All but which of the following help to explain why interest rates vary?
    a. Differences in risk
    b. Differences in degree of liquidity people wish to maintain
    c. The fact that interest rates are set by government
    d. Differences in the competitiveness of capital markets

13. Economists have advanced all but which one of the following to help explain why economic profits exist?
    a. Variations in weather from one region to another
    b. Monopoly power
    c. Risk and uncertainty
    d. Innovation

14. Which of the following is *not* a case of economic discrimination?
    a. Wage determined on the basis of sex
    b. Job determined on the basis of race
    c. Wage difference determined by crowding
    d. Wage difference determined by differences in productivity

15. Steps that have been helpful in beginning to do away with job and wage discrimination have included all but which one of the following?
    a. Civil rights legislation
    b. Pressures of competition
    c. Unionization of women and minorities
    d. Minimum wage legislation designed to help those against whom discrimination is practiced

SECTION C Matching questions

Match the phrases in column B to the terms in column A.

Column A	Column B
1. Crowding	(a) Tradeoffs between more income and more leisure
2. Competitive wage	
3. Monopoly wage	(b) Increases supply of labor in some fields, decreases it in others
4. Minimum wage	
5. Backward-bending curve for labor supply	(c) Rate at which amount of labor supplied changes as wage changes
6. Economic rent	(d) $P_L = VMP_L$
7. Innovation	(e) $P_L = MRP_L$
8. Bilateral monopoly	(f) Decreases employment because it is above the MRP of many laborers
9. Henry George	
10. Elasticity of supply of resource	(g) Payment to a factor that is in perfectly inelastic supply
11. Quasi-rent	(h) One theory as to why economic profit exists
	(i) Wage set between MRP_L and S_L
	(j) Single-tax movement
	(k) Payment to a factor in relatively inelastic supply

ANSWERS

Part 4

Section A   1, F; 2, F; 3, T; 4, T; 5, F; 6, T; 7, T; 8, F; 9, F; 10, F; 11, T; 12, F; 13, T; 14, F; 15, F; 16, T; 17, F; 18, F; 19, F; 20, T; 21, F; 22,T; 23, T; 24, F

Section B   1, *c*; 2, *d*; 3, *c*; 4, *a*; 5, *b*; 6, *d*; 7, *b*; 8, *a*; 9, *c;* 10, *b;* 11, *d,* 12, *c,* 13, *a; 14,d; 15, d*

Section C   1, b; 2, d; 3, e; 4, f; 5, a; 6, g; 7, h; 8, i; 9, j; 10, c; 11, k

CHAPTER 13 *Patterns of International Trade*

Application 13 *Does Trade Create Development?*

PART 1

Reread the sections entitled "Summing Up" at the end of Chapter 13 and Application 13. These provide an excellent review of both chapter and application.

Things to Watch For

Chapter 13

Chapter 13 deals with **exports** (X, those things a nation sells to others) and **imports** (M, those things it buys from others). This trade is made up of **visible items** (the commodities) and **invisible items** (services, including financial services).

Net foreign trade (X-M) can exert a powerful macroeconomic influence on a nation. Net foreign trade is the same as the **balance of trade**.

Trade is important for any nation except a nation that decides to pursue a course of **autarky**, or economic self-sufficiency. Autarky is economically disadvantageous, not in terms of **absolute advantage** (which exists when a given nation can produce all things more efficiently than any other nation can), but in terms of **comparative advantage** (which exists when a given nation can produce *some* things relatively more efficiently than others).

A production-possibilities schedule and a production-possibilities curve show that the internal rate at which a nation gives up one good to produce another ultimately increases. When one looks at these schedules and curves, the advantage to a nation of foreign trade becomes clear. By trading with one another, two nations that operate under comparative advantage can both have more of all goods and services than would be possible without trade.

The reason trade is beneficial is that the internal rate of exchange of one country (the slope of its production-possibilities schedule) is different from that of another country. Trade creates a new exchange rate, different from the internal rates of either nation. The actual exchange rate that is established is called the **terms of trade**. It is the rate at which one nation's goods are exchanged for the goods of another nation. (Later on in the chapter, we see that the terms of trade is also the ratio of the *prices* of exports to the *prices* of imports.)

Note these facts about comparative advantage: (1) Nations have differing comparative advantages based on varying endowments of resources, differing physical features, differing degrees of development of capital markets, and differing ratios of capital to labor. (2) As a nation develops, its comparative advantage changes. The main reason why specialization of trade on the basis of comparative advantage occurs is that a nation that does not practice such specialization encounters increasing costs. That is, a nation that wishes to produce both good A and good B finds that the necessary internal tradeoffs force it to give up larger and larger amounts of one of the two goods. Finally, it gets to the point at which it is cheaper to import some of the goods it would otherwise produce. Trade specialization is not, however, complete. This is so for a number of reasons. (1) International trade may affect the internal level of employment. (2) There is a lack of competition in internal trade. (3) International trade carries certain externalities. (4) Relative prices between one country and another may not reflect scarcities. (5) There is **protectionism**, which means legal or government-established barriers to free trade.

The main devices a government uses to practice protectionism are as follows: (1) **Tariffs**, or taxes on imports. Tariffs reduce the supply of the good that is being so taxed, raise the price of it, increase domestic monopoly power, and raise revenue for the government. (2) **Quotas**, or restrictions on the amounts of certain goods that may be imported. The effects of quotas are the same as those of tariffs, except that quotas do not raise revenue for the government. (3) **Embargoes**, or laws that prohibit the import of certain goods altogether. The effect of embargoes is to reduce the supply of the good to domestic sources, raise the price of the good, and enhance domestic monopoly power. Lack of effective opposition by consumers to import quotas may be attributable to rational ignorance.

The arguments in favor of trade protectionism are (1) the *infant-industry argument,* which holds that a newly begun, developing industry needs to be protected from mature foreign competitors; (2) the *national-security argument,* which holds that a nation should preserve its defense industries against competition from foreign defense materials, because it can never be sure of having a ready supply of any good that must be imported; (3) the *cheap-foreign-labor argument;* and (4) the *macroeconomic-employment argument,* which holds that protectionism restricts imports, stimulates exports, and as a result lowers unemployment.

Economists generally reject all these arguments as being fallacious and self-defeating, except for the national-security argument. Even in that case they feel that direct subsidies to defense industries are preferable to tariffs and quotas and embargoes, because subsidies give a clear picture of the costs involved. Canada has never allowed trade to be entirely free, but it also has only rarely set up extremely high tariffs or embargoes or other very restrictive trade rules.

GATT, the General Agreement on Tarrifs and Trade, was set up in 1947 to foster trade and lower various forms of obstacles to free trade.

Application 13

Application 13 deals with an issue very much in the forefront today. Does international trade help nations (especially the poor nations) to develop economically? The classical economists thought that it does. In fact, they felt that international trade is essential to a nation's economic development. The answer has been made more complicated by the appearance of a number of countries now called newly industrialized countries (NICs) and also the creation in the 70s and 80s of a very serious debt problem for many NICs and less developed countries (LDCs). Application 13 shows that, if one takes a static approach (that is, if one ignores the changes that take place over time), this argument is compelling. Nations that trade will allocate their resources to their most productive uses, and thus will have a greater productivity and higher per capita income than nations that don't trade.

At least five points of doubt have been raised about whether international trade will have the same positive result over time. (1) *Imperfections in the factor market.* As these imperfections disappear, relative costs and comparative advantage change. (2) *Unreliability of export markets.* Some highly specialized raw-material economies are very unstable. They can't grow rapidly because of price and income elasticities of demand for their products. The terms of trade are more unfavorable to them than to the developed industrialized nations. (3) *Changes in productivity.* Manufacturing, even when it is not dictated by comparative advantage, builds up supplies of resources and a pool of labor with sophisticated skills to a much greater degree than agriculture does. (4) *Dynamic external economies.* Equilibrium market prices do not indicate which investments must be taken together to be profitable. Thus, the market signals that emerge when nations trade under the comparative-advantage system may dictate the wrong investments. (5) *Uncertainty and flexibility.* An economy that is diversified in its trade relationships—one that does not base its trade strictly on comparative advantage—can respond more quickly and flexibly to changes in supply and demand (world prices) than an economy that is dependent on one or a few products.

Economists generally disregard the first two of these arguments. But they concede that the others may support an argument for a shift of economic policy away from comparative advantage. Recently, pressures have developed to create a "new economic order," one in which poor nations are given special trading arrangements and concessions. If such concessions are granted, they will probably involve a further move away from comparative advantage. Intense debate continues about whether free trade benefits the NICs and LDCs or whether special treatment should be afforded them to encourage growth.

PART 2

Define the following terms and concepts.

1. Exports
2. Imports
3. Visible items
4. Invisible items
5. Net foreign trade
6. Balance of trade
7. Absolute advantage
8. Comparative advantage
9. Terms of trade
10. Protectionism
11. Tariff
12. Quota
13. Embargo
14. Infant industry agreement
15. Autarky
16. National security agreement
17. Cheap foreign labor agreement
18. Economic development
19. Dynamic external economies
20. Rational ignorance
21. Beggar thy neighbor
22. Newly Industrialized Countries (NICs)
23. GATT

PART 3

Answer the following questions and problems.

1. What problems would nations experience in trying to achieve autarky?

2. Consider the hypothetical production-possibilities schedule for the United States and Canada shown in Table 13-1.
   a. What happens to the rate of exchange of trucks for copper in the United States? of copper for trucks in Canada?
   b. What is the United States' initial rate of exchange of copper for trucks? Canada's initial rate of exchange of trucks for copper?
   c. What causes the internal rate of exchange to change in each of the two countries?
   d. For trade to take place in this case (Canadian copper to the United States, American trucks to Canada), what is the range within which the terms of trade must fall?

Table 13-1 Production-Possibilities Schedules: United States and Canada

United States		Canada	
Units of Trucks	Units of Copper	Units of Trucks	Units of Copper
100	0	0	100
80	10	5	80
60	20	10	60
40	30	15	40
20	40	20	20
0	50	25	0

3. In Figure 13-1, plot the production-possibilities schedules for (a) the United States and (b) Canada from the data in Table 13-1. Then consider the following additions to this economic situation.
   a. What would the production-possibilities curves look like if resources were specialized in their uses?
   b. In Figure 13-1 plot the consumption possibilities *after* trade for both countries.
   c. What causes the internal rate of exchange to change in each of the two countries?

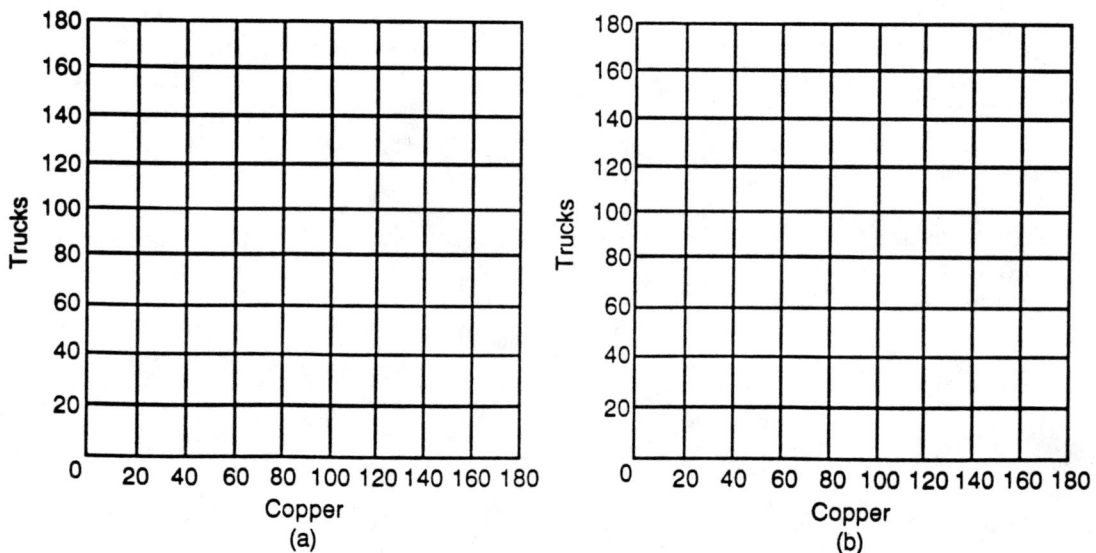

Figure 13-1 Production-Possibilities Curves

d. For trade to take place in this case (Canadian copper to the United States, American trucks to Canada), what is the range within which the terms of trade must fall?
e. Would the United States benefit from trade with Canada even if it had an absolute advantage in producing both trucks and copper? Why?

4. What are the major arguments for protectionism? Why do economists regard all but one as fallacious?

5. Consider Figure 13-2 and then answer the following questions.
   a. What is the equilibrium price of the imported good (including foreign imports)?
   b. Draw a new supply curve reflecting a tariff on this good that *partially* reduces foreign supply. What happens to price? Who bears the burden of the tariff? Who benefits from the tariff?
   c. What will the price of this good be if an embargo is placed on imports of it from abroad? Who benefits from—and who "pays" for—the embargo?

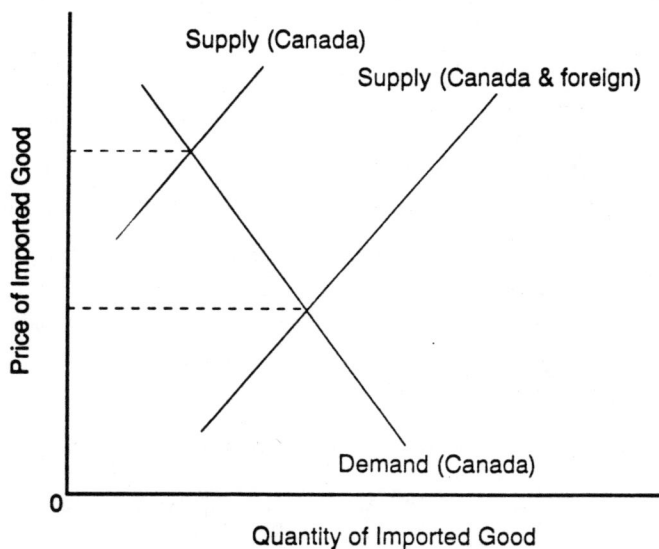

Figure 13-2 Effects of a Tariff

6. Why did the classical economists regard comparative-advantage trade as essential to the economic development of nations?

7. There are several arguments in favor of moving away from comparative advantage as the basis for a developing nation's trade policy. Which ones are regarded by some economists as valid?

8. Explain as convincingly as you can why a free trade agreement with Mexico will benefit Canada.

PART 4 Self-test

SECTION A   True/false questions

T F 1. The balance of trade measures the difference between exports and imports.

T F 2. Foreign trade is not important to Canada.

T F 3. Net foreign trade is equal to exports plus imports.

T F 4. The balance of trade affects the economy through its effects on GNP.

T F 5. A nation that has an *absolute* disadvantage in producing all its goods should not trade with other nations.

T F 6. In a real-world situation, production-possibilities curves are not likely to be straight lines.

T F 7. If internal rates of exchange are the same in two different nations, there is no advantage to be had from trade between them.

T F 8. The terms of trade express the prices at which the goods of one nation can be exchanged for the goods of another nation.

T F 9. The comparative advantage of Canada has changed little over the last century.

T F 10. Externalities may cause specialization of trade among nations to be incomplete.

T F 11. Tariffs decrease domestic monopoly power.

T F 12. The United States has never imposed an embargo in modern times.

T F 13. Economists accept all the arguments in favor of protectionism except the macroeconomic-employment argument.

T F 14. The classical economists saw little need for nations to trade with one another.

T F 15. At any given time, the nation that allocates its resources on the basis of comparative advantage is likely to have a greater output than the one that does not.

T F 16. One reason why nations should follow the principle of comparative advantage is the notion of dynamic external economies, which means that certain investments should be undertaken together.

T F 17. Price and income elasticities of demand may, according to some economists, weigh against raw-material-producing nations' use of trade as a basis for their economic development.

T   F   18. A nation exporting one or just a few commodities is more likely to be able to adjust to changes in international supply and demand than a nation that exports many.

T   F   19. GATT was set up by the U.S. to protect U.S. industry from foreign competition.

SECTION B Multiple-choice questions

1. Which of the following is *not* a visible item of trade?
   a. Automobile exports
   b. Steel imports
   c. Petroleum imports
   d. Payments to foreign shippers

2. The balance of trade is which one of the following?
   a. Exports minus imports
   b. Visible minus invisible items of trade
   c. Exports divided by imports
   d. The balance in the federal budget

3. When imports increase which of the following occurs?
   a. the balance of trade increases
   b. the balance of trade decreases
   c. The balance of trade is unaffected
   d. GNP increases

4. The terms of trade express the relationship between
   a. exports and imports.
   b. total paid for exports and total paid for imports.
   c. prices paid for exports and prices paid for imports.
   d. visible and invisible items of trade.

5. A nation's consumption-possibilities curve is probably affected by international trade in which one of the following ways?
   a. It is greater after trade.
   b. It is less after trade.
   c. It is unaffected by trade.
   d. The effect is indeterminate.

6. One of the following does *not* cause trade specialization to be incomplete. Which?
   a. Increasing costs
   b. Noncompetitive trading conditions
   c. Externalities
   d. Complete factor substitutability

7. Economists do *not* reject which one of the following arguments in favor of protectionism?
   a. Cheap foreign labor
   b. Infant industry
   c. Macroeconomic employment
   d. National security

8. A tariff is *not* likely to do which one of the following?
   a. Reduce domestic prices
   b. Increase domestic supply
   c. Increase government revenues
   d. Increase domestic monopoly power

9. Economists generally accept all but which one of the following reservations about comparative-advantage trade among nations?
   a. Changes in factor cost
   b. Uncertainty and flexibility
   c. Dynamic external economies
   d. Changes in productivity

10. Which of the following changes is least likely to occur in international trade?
    a. Special trading privileges for poor countries
    b. Special borrowing privileges at the IMF for poor countries
    c. Movement in the direction of free trade
    d. Lower tariffs in rich nations for goods imported from poor nations

SECTION C Matching questions

Match the phrases in column B to the terms in column A.

Column A	Column B
1. Autarky	(a) Exports minus imports
2. Absolute advantage	(b) Excludes exports and imports
3. Internal rate of exchange	(c) Economic self-sufficiency
4. Terms of trade	(d) Producing all things more efficiently than others can
5. Net foreign trade	(e) Producing some things more efficiently than others can
6. Tariff	(f) Domestic tradeoff between goods for a nation
7. Embargo	(g) Price of exports ÷ prices of imports
8. Invisible items of trade	(h) Tax on imported goods
9. Dynamic external economies	(i) Prohibition against importing a certain good
10. Comparative advantage	(j) Return greater when a group of investments is taken together

ANSWERS

Part 4

Section A   1, T; 2, F; 3, F; 4, T; 5, F; 6, T; 7, T; 8, T; 9, F; 10, T; 11, F; 12, F; 13, F; 14, F; 15, T; 16, F; 17, T; 18, F; 19, F

Section B   1, *d*; 2, *a*; 3, *b*; 4, *c*; 5, *a*; 6, *d*; 7, *d*; 8, *a*; 9, *a*; 10, *c*

Section C   1, c; 2, d; 3, f; 4, g; 5, a; 6, h; 7, i; 8, b; 9, j; 10, e